SOFT TOYS
MADE EASY

GAIL ATTWELL

SOFT TOYS

MADE EASY

Photography by Janek Szymanowski

NEW HOLLAND

First published in 1993 by
New Holland (Publishers) Ltd
London • Cape Town • Sydney • Singapore

Reprinted 1994 and 1996

24 Nutford Place
London W1H 6DQ
UK

P.O. Box 1144
Cape Town 8000
South Africa

3/2 Aquatic Drive
Frenchs Forest, NSW 2086
Australia

ISBN 1 85368 254 3 (hbk)
ISBN 1 85368 152 0 (pbk)

Editor: Hilda Hermann
Designer: Tracey Carstens
Cover designer: Tracey Carstens
Illustrator: Gail Attwell
Photographer: Janek Szymanowski
Styling: Penny Swift
Phototypeset by Bellset
Originated by Unifoto (Pty) Ltd
Printed and bound in Malaysia by Times Offset (m) sdn Bhd

Contents

Before You Start – Hints To Help You

STUFFING
This comes in many different forms and qualities. After all the care you've taken in making the toy, it would be a pity to stuff it with a cheap material which would give it a lumpy appearance. Foam chips, besides being unsafe, are unsuitable, as is kapok, as neither material can be washed. White polyester makes the best quality stuffing.

Use small amounts of stuffing at a time, continually feeling the outside of the toy to ensure that it is smooth and the stuffing is even. To fill small spaces, push tiny bits of stuffing into position, using the blunt end of a crochet hook (a knitting needle is too sharp).

The most important area to stuff properly is the neck. Stuff the neck firmly, otherwise the head will wobble from side to side.

COLOUR
Choose colours with care. If making a toy as a decorative feature, match fabrics already in the room, for example, those of the duvet cover, curtains and so on.

Contrasting colours and patterns work well – combine purple or lilac with yellow tones, or apricot and orange with blue tones.

GLUE
A glue gun is a wonderful investment – it has many uses in the home besides toy making. Colourless glue in a tube is also suitable, as it creates a neat appearance.

USING BIAS BINDING
Open out one folded edge of the bias binding. Pin the binding to the wrong side of the edge to be bound, with the crease of the binding on the seam line. Stitch the binding to the edge along the crease. Turn the binding to the front of the edge, to cover the previous stitching line, and stitch neatly in place, close to the folded edge of the binding.

FABRIC
Preferably use new fabric when making toys, for a crisp, fresh look.

Fabric for bodies and heads can vary. Fine, brushed nylon is recommended, using the wrong side as the right side. The fabric has some stretch, and is a good base on which to embroider, paint or glue a face. When sewing body pieces together, use a stretch stitch, so set your sewing machine on to a very slight zig-zag stitch.

For clothing, use fabric suitable for the type of toy being made.

FUR FABRIC
This is easy to work with and can hide less than perfect stitching. First check that your sewing machine can cope with sewing through the thickness.

Always trace the pattern on to the back of the fabric with the pile of the fur in the direction indicated on the pattern. Flip over the pattern piece when you have to cut a left and a right piece.

Cut only one thickness at a time, snipping through the woven back of the fabric to avoid cutting through the pile.

After sewing a fur piece, be sure to remove all pins and after turning through the fabric, check for any pile caught in the seams. If necessary, gently run the point of a pin or needle over the seam to release the pile.

When glueing on features such as eyes, trim pile away from the area first.

HAIR
Double knitting wool or 4-ply is the most suitable, and wool with a brushed effect looks good.

1. *For sew-on curls,* wind the wool round as many fingers as necessary to give the required length of a curl.

2. Wind the wool round your fingers as many times as necessary to give the desired thickness of a curl.

3. Cut off the wool, slip the curl off your fingers and stitch twice through the loops of the wool to the head of the toy.

4. Pull the stitches tight and sew the curls next to each other on the head. The curls are normally longer at the back and sides, and shorter at the front of the head.

1. *To make strips of curls,* use a length of 6 mm-wide (¼ in-wide) tape.

2. With your sewing machine set on a close stitch, sew a few stitches down the centre of the tape at one end.

3. Wind the wool round your fingers to give the desired length and thickness of curl, remembering that the length of these curls will be half the length you wind round your fingers.

4. Cut the wool, slip the curls off your fingers and position them across the width of the tape. Sew through the middle of the curls.

5. Repeat the procedure until you have a sufficient length of curl-covered tape to make the desired hairstyle.

6. Sew a second row of stitching over the first to strengthen. Sew the tape neatly to the head as required.

7. You can cut through the loops to give a different effect.

ROUGE
Powder rouge, available at any cosmetic counter, is ideal. The rouge does wash out, but is easily touched up.

1. Using the brush provided, start in the centre of the cheek, and brush lightly with a circular motion.

2. Continue adding more rouge until the desired effect is achieved.

NOSES

Stand-out noses are made by cutting a circle of fabric which has some stretch. You can also make a small pompon or glue on a felt nose.

A 7 cm (2¾ in) diameter fabric circle is the usual size unless otherwise stated.

Run a gathering thread round the outer edge. Put a small ball of stuffing into the centre of the wrong side of the fabric, pull up the gathers tightly to secure, and sew the nose in position.

FELT

Felt is usually bought in squares. Use a good quality felt as the very thin version is not suitable for making shoes or body parts for toys.

When cutting out small pieces of felt, first brush the back of the felt with a little white craft glue and let it dry thoroughly. The glue backing will give small pieces of felt a smooth edge when you cut them out. Bigger pieces of felt should be sewn and not glued on to a toy.

FACES

A beautifully made toy can be spoilt by an ugly face. The less facial detail, the more effective, so don't add too many freckles, eyelashes and so on.

Pin the felt pieces on to the face first, to achieve a pleasing effect. Eyes normally look best if positioned halfway down the face. A sparkle can be added to the eye with a little dot of white felt, or waterproof white paint.

When embroidering facial detail, use three strands of cotton.

THREAD

Strong thread is necessary for certain parts of toy making, especially when pulling up gathers tightly.

POMPON

The size of each pompon varies depending on the size of the toy. The method is identical for each one: only the diameter of the circles and the amount of wool used will change.

You will need a compass, pencil, pair of scissors, a needle, some wool, cotton thread, and thin cardboard.

1. Use a compass to draw two circles with a diameter of the pompon required, on thin card.

2. Cut a hole measuring approximately 8 mm (⅜ in) in diameter in the centre of each circle.

3. Thread a needle with two strands of wool and, holding the two circles together, wind the wool round the circles, passing the needle through the hole each time.

4. Continue winding wool round, cutting off the wool at the outer edge of the circles as it runs out.

5. Rethread the needle with more wool and continue winding in this way until the centre hole is full and the circles are well covered.

6. Snip through the wool, all the way round, between the circles.

7. Slide a length of strong cord or cotton thread between the two circles of cardboard, wind it tightly round the centre of the pompon a couple of times and tie the ends firmly.

8. Leave the long ends of cotton for attaching the pompon to the toy.

9. Cut the card carefully to the centre and twist the card circles out of the pompon. Fluff out the pompon and trim the ends if necessary.

Elephant caddy

This makes a wonderful baby shower gift, holding a dummy on the trunk, safety pins through the ears and a saddle bag with cream or a brush. The elephant would look equally good made in primary colours. It is 44 cm (17 ³⁄₈ in) long, excluding the tail.

REQUIREMENTS

65 cm x 90 cm (25½ in x 35½ in) of fake fur fabric for the body, ears and tail

15 cm x 46 cm (6 in x 18⅛ in) of fabric for the ear linings

Polyester stuffing

Scrap of long-pile fake fur for the tail tip (optional)

50 cm (19¾ in) of 33 mm (1¼ in) wide ribbon

Scraps of black and white felt for the eyes

Glue

50 cm x 30 cm (19¾ in x 12 in) of fabric for the saddle bag

2 press studs

1. *To make the body*, transfer the patterns on pages 66 and 67 on to tracing paper and cut out. Pin the traced pattern to the fur fabric and cut out two body pieces and two underbody pieces.

2. With right sides together, sew the underbody pieces along the centre seam, leaving a gap in the seam as indicated on the pattern.

3. With right sides together, sew the body pieces from point A round the trunk and down the back to point B as indicated on the pattern. Trim excess seam allowance from the trunk.

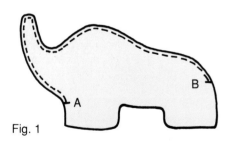

Fig. 1

4. With right sides together, sew the underbody piece to the body piece from point A to point B, and round the other side of the body, back to point A. Clip into the curves and turn through. Stuff the body firmly and sew the gap in the seam closed.

5. *To make the ears*, transfer the ear pattern on page 66 on to tracing paper and cut out. Pin the traced pattern to the fabric and cut out two pieces from the fake fur fabric and two pieces from the lining fabric.

6. With right sides together, sew an ear lining piece to each fake fur fabric ear, leaving the body edge open. Turn through. Turn in the raw edges at the body edge, and sew them together neatly, pulling up the stitches to gather the fabric pieces slightly.

7. Sew the ears to the body neatly, in the positions indicated on the pattern.

8. *To make the tail*, transfer the tail pattern on page 67 on to tracing paper and cut out. Pin the traced pattern to the fake fur fabric and cut out two pieces.

9. With right sides together, sew the tail pieces together, leaving the body edge open. Turn through.

10. Sew a 6 cm x 3 cm (2⅓ in x 1¼ in) strip of long-pile fake fur fabric round the tail end (optional).

11. Sew the tail to the body, in the position indicated on the pattern.

12. *To make the saddle bag*, cut two strips of fabric, each measuring 50 cm x 10 cm (19¾ in x 4 in). Cut two pocket pieces each measuring 10 cm x 10 cm (4 in x 4 in).

13. Hem one edge of each pocket piece, turning under 5 mm (¼ in) then 5 mm (¼ in) again. Turn under 1 cm (⅜ in) along the opposite (bottom) edge and tack in place.

14. With right sides up, position the bottom edge of each pocket piece 12 cm (4¾ in) from the raw edges of one of the long strips of fabric and sew as shown in fig. 2.

15. With right sides together, sew the two long strips together, leaving one short edge open. Turn through. Turn in the raw edges of the open end and sew them closed. Topstitch all round the edge, close to the edge.

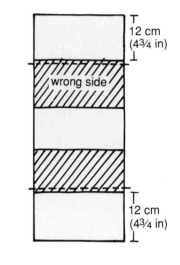

12 cm (4¾ in)

wrong side

12 cm (4¾ in)

Fig. 2

16. Fit the saddle bag on the elephant, overlapping the ends under the tummy, and marking the position at each corner for the press studs. Sew the press studs in place.

17. Cut the eyes from the white and black felt. Mark their position on the face. Trim the fur at the eye positions and glue the eyes in place.

18. Make a bow from the ribbon and glue it to the top of the head.

Fig. 3 Full-size eye

Mother Goose nappy holder

Use Mother Goose to hold nappies or kitchen towels. Dressed in fabric to match your colour scheme, she also adds a touch of humour to a room.

REQUIREMENTS

24 cm x 34 cm (9½ in x 13½ in)of firm cardboard for the base
1 m (1 yd 3 in) of 150 cm (60 in) wide fabric for the skirt, bodice, bonnet, base and frills
34 cm x 55 cm (13½ in x 21⅝ in) of white fabric for the head and wings
Polyester stuffing
Glue
12 cm x 20 cm (4¾ in x 7⅞ in) of orange fabric for the beak
32 cm (12⅝ in) of 15 mm (¾ in) wide lace
60 cm (23⅝ in) of 8 mm (⅜ in) wide ribbon
62 cm x 16 cm (24½ in x 6¼ in) of fabric for the scarf
Scraps of black felt for the eyes
Black waterproof felt-tipped pen
12 cm (4¾ in) of tape or ribbon for the hanging loop
2 small buttons
2 x 3.5 cm (1½ in) diameter metal or plastic rings for the glasses
Strong thread
26 cm (10¾ in) of narrow elastic

1. Cut the nappy holder fabric as follows: 102 cm x 40 cm (40½ in x 15¾ in) for the skirt piece, 26 cm x 36 cm (10¾ in x 14¼ in) for the base, 2 pieces each 75 cm x 6 cm (29½ in x 2⅓ in) for the frills, 70 cm x 26.5 cm (28 in x 10½ in) to cover the cardboard base, 2 pieces each 22 cm x 16 cm (8⅝ in x 6¼ in) for the bodice.

2. *To cover the cardboard base*, fold the 70 cm x 26.5 cm (28 in x 10½ in) piece of fabric in half, with right sides together. Sew along the sides of the fabric as shown in fig. 1, to form a pocket.

3. Turn through, and slip the cardboard base into the pocket. Turn in the raw edges and sew them together to enclose the cardboard.

4. *To make the frills*, hem one long edge of each frill piece.

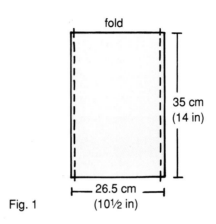

fold

35 cm
(14 in)

26.5 cm
(10½ in)

Fig. 1

5. Run a gathering thread along the other long edges. Pull up the gathers evenly to measure 40 cm (15¾ in).

6. With right sides together, sew the frills to the 40 cm (15¾ in) edges of the skirt section as shown in fig. 2.

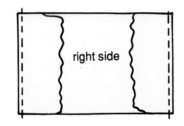

right side

Fig. 2

7. Fold the seam allowances of the frills on to the skirt and topstitch in place, on the right side, close to the seam, as shown in fig. 3.

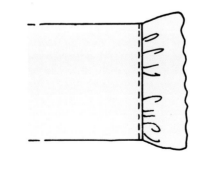

Fig. 3

8. *To attach the skirt to the fabric base*, mark the centre of one long edge of the skirt section. Mark the centre of one long edge of the 26 cm x 36 cm (10¾ in x 14¼ in) base piece.

9. With right sides together, matching the two centre points, pin the skirt section to the base piece. Make a small pleat in the skirt section at each corner to ease the fabric round the corners neatly. There will be a 13 cm (5⅛ in) space between the frills at the front of the base.

10. Sew the skirt to the base and topstitch in place, close to the seam. Hem the open space between the frills at the front.

11. *To make the wings*, transfer the wing pattern on page 68 on to tracing paper and cut out. Pin the traced pattern to the white fabric and cut out four wing pieces.

12. With right sides together, join the wings in pairs, leaving the bodice edge open. Clip into the curves of the wings and turn through.

13. Stuff the wings. Topstitch round the outer edge, 5 mm (¼ in) from the edge and sew the raw edges together.

14. *To make the head*, transfer the head and beak patterns on page 68 on to tracing paper and cut out. Pin the traced head pattern to the white fabric and cut out two pieces. Pin the traced beak pattern to the orange fabric and cut out two pieces.

15. With right sides together, sew a beak piece to each head piece. With right sides together, join the two head pieces together, leaving the neck edge open. Clip into the curves and turn through.

16. Stuff the head firmly. Run a gathering thread round the neck edge, pull up the gathers tightly and sew off securely.

17. *To make the bodice*, pin and tack the wings to the right side of one of the bodice pieces, as shown in fig. 4.

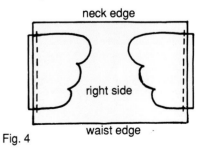

neck edge

right side

waist edge

Fig. 4

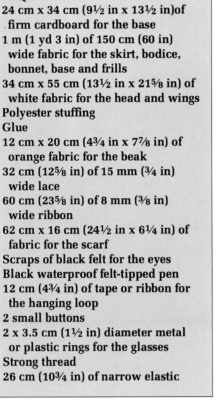

18. With right sides together, join the bodice pieces together, along the length of the side seams, incorporating the wings into the seams.

19. Overlap the frills on the skirt section and pin them together. Run a gathering thread round the top edge of the skirt section. Pull up the gathers evenly across the top of the skirt section, until it fits across the width of the bodice, as shown in fig. 5.

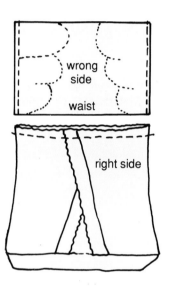

Fig. 5

20. Pin, tack and sew the gathered edges of the skirt section together, to keep the gathers in place.

21. With right sides together, slip the skirt section into the bodice, with the gathered edge of the skirt section level with the waist edge of the bodice.

22. Pin in position and sew across, through all the layers of fabric, as shown in fig. 6.

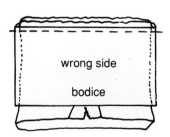

Fig. 6

23. Turn through and remove the gathering thread. Stuff the bodice.

24. Turn in a 1 cm (⅜ in) hem along the neck edge of the bodice and run a gathering thread round it.

25. Insert the head into the bodice, pull up the gathers tightly round the neck and sew the bodice neck edge to the gooses neck very securely.

26. *To make the bonnet*, transfer the bonnet pattern on page 68 on to tracing paper and cut out. Pin the traced pattern to the fabric and cut out two pieces.

27. With right sides together, join the bonnet pieces along the curved edge.

28. Sew the length of lace to the right side of the face edge of the bonnet as shown in fig. 7.

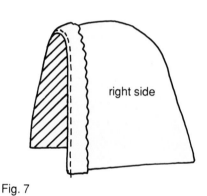

Fig. 7

29. Fold the lace forward, press the seam allowance to the inside of the bonnet and topstitch in place, on the right side, close to the edge.

30. Cut a 14 cm (5½ in) length of narrow elastic and, starting and ending 1 cm (⅜ in) from the neck edge at each side, use a zig-zag stitch to sew the elastic to the inside of the face edge of the bonnet, stretching the elastic as you sew.

31. Hem the neck edge of the bonnet by turning in 5 mm (¼ in) then 8 mm (⅜ in).

32. Cut a 12 cm (4¾ in) length of narrow elastic and sew it to the inside of the neck edge of the bonnet in the same manner as for the face edge.

33. Sew a 20 cm (7⅞ in) length of 8 mm (⅜ in) wide ribbon to each corner of the bonnet for ties.

34. Cut out two eyes from black felt and glue in place. Mark the eyelashes with a black waterproof felt-tipped pen.

35. *To make the glasses*, tie the two rings together and sew them to the top of the beak at each side.

36. Stuff the bonnet lightly and tie it on to the head.

37. Sew two buttons to the centre front of the bodice.

38. Make a bow from 20 cm (7⅞ in) of 8 mm (⅜ in) wide ribbon and glue it to the centre front of the waist.

39. *To make the scarf*, cut the fabric as shown in fig. 8. Leave the fabric unhemmed and tie it loosely round the neck of the goose.

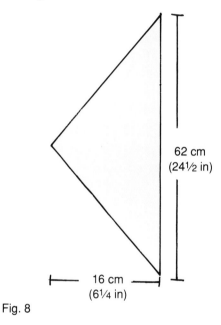

Fig. 8

40. Sew a loop of tape to the centre back seam of the neck to hang the holder.

41. Insert the covered cardboard base in the bottom of the skirt section.

Fig. 9 Full-size eye

Humpty Dumpty bib

Make mealtimes fun with this bib and its detachable Humpty Dumpty. Turn him into a finger puppet by sewing a loop of elastic to the back of the body.

7. Tack the arms to the right side of one of the body pieces as shown in fig. 1.

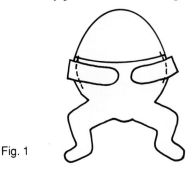

Fig. 1

1. *To make the bib*, transfer the bib patterns on page 69 on to tracing paper and cut out. Pin the traced cloud patterns, wrong side up, to a double layer of white fabric. Draw lightly around the outline. Sew along the dotted line indicated on the pattern, leaving the bib edge open. Cut out the clouds and clip into the curves. Turn through.

2. Cut out the blue, yellow and green sections of the bib. Pin, tack and sew the clouds in position on the blue section. With right sides together, sew the yellow section to the blue section and the green section to the yellow section. Press the seams flat. Sew the soft half of the velcro to the bib as indicated on the pattern.

3. Pin the bib, right side up, to the face cloth. Stitch together along the two seam lines between the three sections. Stitch close to the edge, round the fabric pieces, including the neck edge. Cut away excess face cloth.

4. Bind the outer edge using the bias binding. Mark the centre of the bib neck edge and the centre of a 90 cm (35½ in) length of bias-binding. Matching these marks, bind the neck edge, thus leaving equal lengths of binding at each side for the tie ends.

5. *To make Humpty Dumpty*, transfer the Humpty Dumpty patterns on page 69 on to tracing paper and cut out. Pin the traced face pattern to the flesh fabric and cut two pieces. Pin the traced body pattern to the red-spot fabric and cut two pieces. Pin the traced shoe pattern to the black fabric and cut four pieces. Fold the remaining red-spot fabric in half, trace round the arm pattern twice, and sew around the outer edge of each arm, leaving the body edge open. Cut round the edge, turn through and stuff the arms.

6. Using 5 mm (¼ in) seams, with right sides together, sew the face pieces to the body pieces. With right sides together, sew a shoe piece to each ankle edge. Using three strands of red embroidery cotton, embroider the mouth.

8. With right sides together, sew the body pieces together round the outer edge, leaving a gap in the seam as indicated on the pattern, incorporating the arms into the seam. Clip into the curves and turn through. Stuff the Humpty Dumpty firmly, and sew the gap in the seam closed. Topstitch across the top of both legs where they join the body.

9. Cut the nose and cheeks from felt, and glue in position. Glue on the wobbly eyes. Sew the other half of the velcro to the centre back of the body. Make a small bow from the ribbon and glue it to the centre front of the neckline. Glue the sequins on the centre front of the body.

Old McDonald glove puppets

Children will love entertaining each other with these puppets and making the appropriate animal noises. Using the basic body shape, make other animals to add to the set.

REQUIREMENTS

Glue

PIG
24 cm x 38 cm (9 ½ in x 15 in) of pink fabric for the body
Scraps of pink and black felt for the ears, snout and trotters
Scrap of 8 mm (⅜ in) wide ribbon
1 pair of small wobbly eyes

DUCK
24 cm x 38 cm (9 ½ in x 15 in) of yellow fabric for the body
Scraps of black and orange felt for the eyes and beak
Black waterproof felt-tipped pen
1 yellow feather
Scrap of 8 mm (⅜ in) wide ribbon

COW
24 cm x 38 cm (9 ½ in x 15 in) of white fabric for the body
Scraps of pink, beige, black, white and brown felt
1 pair of small wobbly eyes
14 cm (5 ½ in) of 8 mm (⅜ in) wide ribbon
1 small bell

OLD McDONALD
20 cm x 16 cm (7 ⅞ in x 6 ¼ in) of red fabric for the shirt
33 cm x 11 cm (13 in x 4 ⅜ in) of denim fabric for the dungarees
Off-cuts of flesh-coloured, pink, yellow and red felt
32 cm (12 ⅝in) of 8 mm (⅜ in) wide ribbon
1 pair of small wobbly eyes
Scrap of brown fake fur fabric
Red embroidery cotton

PIG

1. To make the pig, transfer the patterns on page 70 on to tracing paper and cut out. Pin the traced body pattern to the pink fabric and cut out two pieces. Pin the traced ear and snout patterns to the pink felt and cut out two ears and one snout. Pin the trotter pattern to the black felt and cut two pieces.

2. Tack the ears to the right side of one body piece at the position indicated on the pattern. Stitch the trotters, along the straight edge, to the right side of the body front piece, at the position indicated on the pattern. (*See* Fig. 1.)

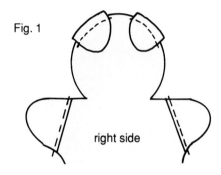

Fig. 1

right side

3. With right sides together, join the body pieces around the outer edge, incorporating the ears and the trotters into the seam, leaving the wrist edge open.

4. Clip into the curves and turn through. Hem the wrist edge by turning in 5 mm (¼ in) then 5 mm (¼ in) again.

5. Fold the ears over and glue the ends to the front of the head.

6. Glue on the snout and the wobbly eyes.

7. Make a bow from the 8 mm (⅜ in) wide ribbon and glue it to the neck at the centre front.

DUCK

1. Transfer the patterns on page 70 on to tracing paper and cut out. Pin the traced body pattern to the yellow fabric and cut two pieces. Cut one beak from orange felt and two eyes from black felt.

2. With right sides together, sew the body pieces round the outer edge, leaving the wrist edge open.

3. Clip into the curves and turn through.

4. Hem the wrist edge by turning in 5 mm (¼ in) then 5 mm (¼ in) again.

5. Glue the beak and eyes in position. Mark the eyelashes with a black water-proof felt-tipped pen.

6. Make a bow from the ribbon and glue it to one side of the neck.

7. Glue a feather to the top of the head at the back.

COW

1. Transfer the patterns on page 70 on to tracing paper and cut out. Pin the traced body pattern to the white fabric and cut two pieces. Cut two inner ears and one nose from pink felt, two outer ears from beige felt, and two hoofs and two nostrils from black felt.

2. Glue a pink inner ear to each beige outer ear, with straight edges level. Fold over one-third of each ear at the base and tack them in place on the right side of one body piece, as for the pig, in the position indicated on the pattern.

3. Sew the hoofs to the right side of the body front along the straight edges, at the position indicated on the pattern.

4. Thread the bell to the centre of the ribbon. Tack the ends of the ribbon to the right side of the body front piece, at each side of the neck.

5. With right sides together, join the body pieces round the outer edge, incorporating the ears, hoofs, and neck ribbon into the seam, leaving the wrist edge open.

6. Clip into the curves and turn through.

7. Hem the wrist edge by turning in 5 mm (¼ in), then 5 mm (¼ in) again.

8. Trace the horn pattern on to a double layer of white felt. Sew around the outline, then cut out the horn, close to the stitching line.

9. Sew the horns to the centre of the head, between the ears.

10. Glue on the nose and the nostrils. Glue on the wobbly eyes.

11. Cut three irregular shapes from the beige and brown felt and glue them to the body.

OLD McDONALD

1. Transfer the patterns on page 70 on to tracing paper and cut out. Pin the traced patterns to the fabrics and cut out two head pieces and two hands from the flesh-coloured felt; two shirt pieces from the red fabric; two dungaree pieces and one bib piece, measuring 9 cm x 7 cm (3½ in x 2¾ in), from the denim; and two hat pieces from the yellow felt.

2. Sew the hands to the right side of the shirt front piece, along the straight edges.

3. Turn in 5 mm (¼ in) along the two 7 cm (2¾ in) edges of the dungaree bib piece, and tack in place. Sew the bib

piece along the hemmed sides to the shirt front piece. Be sure to remove all of the tacking threads.

4. With right sides together, sew a head piece to each shirt piece.

5. With right sides together, join the shirt pieces to the lower body pieces.

6. Sew a hat piece to the right side of the head front and back pieces, along the lower edge of the hat.

7. Join the body pieces round the outer edge, leaving the wrist edge open. Clip into the curves and turn through.

8. Hem the wrist edge by turning in 5 mm (¼ in), then 5 mm (¼ in) again.

9. Cut a nose from red felt and glue it in place. Using two strands of red embroidery cotton, embroider the mouth. Cut two cheeks from pink felt and glue them in place. Glue on the wobbly eyes.

10. Glue a strip of fake fur round the front of the head, at the base of the hat, from ear to ear.

11. Glue the 8 mm (⅜ in) wide ribbon round the neck, with the join at centre front. Make a bow from the remaining ribbon and glue it over the join.

Worm glove puppet

Entertain and delight children (and adults) with this amusing worm. His facial expressions are endless.

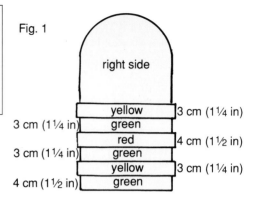

Fig. 1

right side

3 cm (1¼ in)	yellow	3 cm (1¼ in)
	green	
3 cm (1¼ in)	red	4 cm (1½ in)
	green	
	yellow	3 cm (1¼ in)
4 cm (1½ in)	green	

REQUIREMENTS
38 cm x 36 cm (15 in x 14¼ in) of green fabric for the body
8 cm x 18 cm (3⅛ in x 7 in) of yellow spotted fabric
5 cm x 18 cm (2 in x 7 in) of red dotted fabric
22 cm x 19 cm (8⅝ in x 7½ in) of red fabric for the mouth
Glue
Scraps of red and white felt
1 pair of 18 mm (¾ in) diameter wobbly eyes
Buttons to decorate

1. *To make the worm*, transfer the body and mouthpiece pattern on page 71 on to tracing paper and cut out. Pin the traced body pattern to the green fabric and cut out two pieces. Pin the traced mouthpiece pattern to the red fabric and cut one mouthpiece, on the fold.

2. Mark the fold-line on the mouthpiece, at each side, with pins.

3. Cut the stripes as follows: four yellow spotted fabric stripes, each measuring 4 cm x 18 cm (1½ in x 7 in); two red dotted fabric stripes, each measuring 5 cm x 18 cm (2 in x 7 in).

4. Turn in and tack in place a 5 mm (¼ in) hem along each long edge of each striped piece of material.

5. Pin the stripes on to each body piece, to match exactly at the sides, as shown in fig. 1., and sew in place.

6. With right sides together, pin and sew one half of the mouthpiece, from pin to pin, to one of the body pieces, as shown in fig. 2.

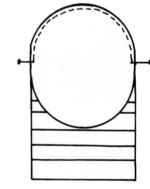

Fig. 2

7. With right sides together, sew the other half of the worm's mouthpiece to the other body piece.

8. Fold the mouthpiece in half, so that the mouth is 'closed'. With right sides together, join the two body pieces by starting at the wrist edge and sewing along the side seam, and just over the fold of the mouthpiece, to catch the fold in the seam. Reinforce the stitching over the fold at each side of the mouth.

9. Turn through. Using a zig-zag stitch, topstitch round the mouth opening, 8 mm (⅜ in) from the edge.

10. Oversew the edges of the mouth together at each side for 2 cm (¾ in) from the corners.

11. Hem the lower edge of the body.

12. Cut eyes from the red and the white felt. Glue them in place. Glue on the wobbly eyes.

13. Sew some buttons to the worm's back to decorate.

Apple place mat

The little mouse finger puppet is good entertainment for problem eaters.

REQUIREMENTS

35 cm (14 in) square of red fabric
40 cm (15¾ in) square of batting
40 cm (15¾ in) square of backing
  fabric, like towelling
8 cm x 8.5 cm (3⅛ in x 3⅜ in) piece
  of fabric for the pocket
Green felt off-cut
Grey felt off-cut
Scraps of pink and white felt
20 cm (7⅞ in) of thin grey cord
1 pink bead
1 pair of small wobbly eyes
Ribbon scrap
Polyester filling
Glue
1 m (1 yd 3 in) of 12 mm (½ in)
  wide red bias binding
Red, green and white sewing thread

1. *To make the place mat*, transfer the apple, leaf and 'shine' patterns on page 71 on to tracing paper and cut out. Pin the traced apple pattern to the red fabric and cut out one piece. Pin the traced leaf pattern on to the green felt and cut one piece. Pin the traced 'shine' pattern to the white felt and cut one piece.

2. Lay the batting on top of the backing fabric, and the apple piece on top of the batting, right side up. Using a zig-zag stitch, stitch the three layers together, all the way round the outer edge of the apple, very close to the edge. Trim away excess batting and backing. Bind the outer edge of the apple.

3. Pin the leaf and the 'shine' in position on the apple and appliqué in place, using a close zig-zag stitch, and green and white cotton respectively, sewing the leaf stem at the same time.

4. *To make the pocket*, turn under a 5 mm (¼ in) double hem along one 8 cm (3⅛ in) edge, and sew in place. Turn under 5 mm (¼ in) all round the other three edges and tack in place. Pin the pocket on the place mat, with the double hemmed edge at the top. Topstitch in place leaving the upper edge open.

5. *To make the mouse*, transfer the mouse patterns on page 71 on to tracing paper and cut out. Pin the traced body and ear patterns to the grey felt and cut two of each. Cut two inner ear pieces from pink felt and one snout from white felt. Glue the pink inner ears to the grey ears, keeping the straight edges level.

6. Cut an 8 cm (3⅛ in) length of grey cord for each arm. Cut a 12 cm (4¾ in) length of grey cord for the tail. Tie a knot at one end of each length. Sew the body pieces together, incorporating he ears and the unknotted ends of the arms and the tail in the positions shown on the pattern, leaving the bottom body edge open.

7. Stuff the head of the mouse up to the neck level. Run a gathering thread round the neck. Pull up the gathers slightly and sew off securely.

Fig. 1

8. Glue on the snout. Sew the pink bead to the top edge of the snout. Glue on the wobbly eyes. Tie the ribbon in a bow round the neck.

Dutch doll

Dressed in her national costume, this doll is a delight for adults as well as children. She is 63 cm (24 ¾ in) tall and all her clothing, except for her hat, is removable.

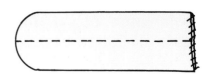

Fig. 3

REQUIREMENTS

40 cm x 44 cm (15¾ in x 17⅜ in) of flesh coloured stretch fabric, with the most stretch going along the 40 cm (15¾ in) edge for the body and arms

2 pieces of black T-shirting, each measuring 26 cm x 12 cm (10¾ in x 4¾ in) with the most stretch going along the 12 cm (4¾ in) edge for the legs

26 cm x 20 cm (10¾ in x 7⅞ in) of beige felt for the clogs

60 cm x 30 cm (23⅝ in x 12 in) of white fabric for the pantaloons

1 m (1 yd 3 in) of 5 mm (¼ in) elastic for the pantaloons and skirt

92 cm x 15 cm (36¼ in x 6 in) of white fabric for the blouse

Scrap of bias binding for the neck of the blouse

Lace trim for the blouse and the apron

3 small press studs

2 tiny buttons for the blouse

26.5 cm x 72 cm (10½ in x 28½ in) of fabric for the skirt

56 cm x 15 cm (22 in x 6 in) of black fabric for the bolero

135 cm (54 in) of bias binding for the bolero

1 large button for the bolero

1 large press stud

Fabric off-cuts in white and a contrast for the apron

32 cm x 60 cm (12⅝ in x 23⅝ in) of white fabric and vilene for the hat

Wool for the hair

Scraps of black, green and red felt

Red embroidery cotton

Black waterproof felt-tipped pen

Rouge

Glue

Polyester filling

50 cm (19¾ in) of 8 mm (⅜ in) ribbon for the plaits

1. *To make the doll's body and arms*, cut the flesh-coloured stretch fabric as shown in fig. 1. With right sides together,

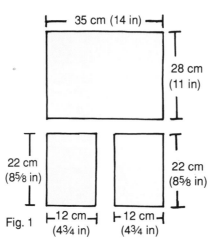

Fig. 1

join the two long edges of the body piece. Turn through. Run a gathering thread round one raw edge, pull up the gathers tightly and sew off securely.

2. With right sides together, fold the arm pieces in half lengthwise and sew as shown in fig. 2. Trim excess fabric and turn through.

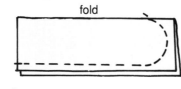

fold

Fig. 2

3. Stuff the body tube to measure approximately 35 cm (14 in) round. Fold the raw edges at the bottom edge of the tube in neatly, and sew closed. Measure 16 cm (6¼ in) down from the gathered top edge of the body and tie a piece of strong thread around the tube at this level to form the neck and head. Don't tie it too tightly or the head will wobble.

4. Stuff the arms to measure approximately 14.5 cm (5¾ in) round, leaving the top 5 cm (2 in) of each arm unstuffed. Centre the seam, fold in the raw edges and sew the top of each arm closed, pulling up the stitches to gather slightly as shown in fig. 3. Sew off securely and sew an arm to each side of the body at shoulder level.

5. *To make the hands*, measure 4.5 cm (1¾ in) from the end of each arm, tie strong thread around the arms, and sew the ends off neatly.

6. *To make the legs*, fold the black T-shirting in half lengthwise, with right sides together. Sew in a similar way as the arm, as shown in fig. 2. Trim excess fabric and turn through. Stuff the legs to measure approximately 14 cm (5½ in) round. Centre the seam, fold in the raw edges all round, and sew the open edge of each leg closed.

7. Sew the legs to the body bottom, over the body bottom seam, with the seams of the legs to the back.

8. *To make the clogs*, transfer the pattern on page 73 on to tracing paper and cut out. Pin the traced pattern to the felt and cut out four clog pieces.

9. Join the clog pieces in pairs, leaving the ankle edge open, using a 5 mm (¼ in) seam. Turn through and stuff.

10. Push the ends of the legs into the clogs, matching the back seams, and pin in place. Sew the clogs neatly on to the legs, turning in a small hem as you sew.

11. *To make the pantaloons*, transfer the pattern on page 72 on to tracing paper and cut out. Pin the traced pattern on to white fabric and cut two pantaloon pieces on the fold.

12. Hem the lower edge of each piece, turning in 5 mm (¼ in), then 5 mm (¼ in) again. With right sides together, join the centre seams. Clip into the curves. With right sides together, sew the inside leg seams together. Clip into the curve and turn through.

13. Hem the waist edge, turning in 5 mm (¼ in) then 1 cm (⅜ in), leaving a gap in the hem for threading the elastic. Measure and cut a length of elastic to fit snugly around the body plus 1 cm (⅜ in).

Thread the elastic through the gap in the hem, overlap the elastic ends by 5 mm (¼ in) and sew them together. Adjust the gathers evenly round the waist edge and sew the gap in the seam closed.

14. Cut two 13 cm (5⅛ in) lengths of elastic, and, using a zig-zag stitch, sew the elastic to the inside of each pantaloon leg, 2 cm (¾ in) from the lower edge, stretching the elastic as you sew.

15. *To make the blouse*, transfer the patterns on pages 72 and 73 on to tracing paper and cut out. Pin the traced patterns to the white fabric and cut out one front on the fold, two backs and two sleeves.

16. With right sides together, join the shoulder seams. Run a gathering thread along the top edge of the sleeve, between the two dots and adjust the gathers evenly. With right sides together, pin, tack and sew the sleeves to the armhole edges of the bodice piece. Clip into the curves and turn through.

17. Sew two lengths of lace trim to the front of the bodice, leaving a gap of 1.5 cm (¾ in) between the two lengths as shown in fig. 4. At the centre back edge of each piece, turn in 5 mm (¼ in) then 1.5 cm (¾ in) and sew in place. Bind the neck of the bodice with bias binding.

Fig. 4

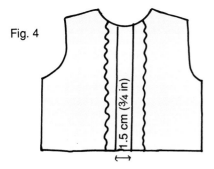

1.5 cm (¾ in)

18. Hem the lower edge of the sleeves and sew on a length of lace trim. With right sides together, sew the underarm seams, from the sleeve edge to the lower edge of the blouse. Sew two tiny buttons to the centre front of the blouse. Sew three press studs to the blouse back.

19. *To make the skirt*, join the short edges of the fabric with the right sides together. Hem one raw edge, by turning in 5 mm (¼ in) then 5 mm (¼ in) again. Hem the other (waist) edge by turning in 5 mm (¼ in) then 1 cm (⅜ in) and leaving a gap in the hem for threading elastic.

20. Cut a length of elastic to fit snugly round the waist of the doll, over the pantaloons and blouse plus 1 cm (⅜ in). Thread the length of elastic through the gap in the hem of the skirt, overlap the elastic ends by 5 mm (¼ in) and sew the elastic ends together. Adjust the gathers evenly round the doll's skirt and sew the gap in the hem closed.

21. *To make the bolero*, transfer the patterns on page 72 on to tracing paper and cut out. Pin the traced patterns to the black fabric and cut one back on the fold and two fronts.

22. With right sides together, join the shoulder seams and side seams. Using bias binding, bind the entire outer edge and armholes. Place the bolero on the doll, overlap the fronts, and mark the correct position for a press stud. Sew on a press stud. Sew a large decorative button to the front overlap.

23. *To make the apron*, cut a piece of white fabric 16 cm x 10 cm (6¼ in x 4 in). Cut a piece of contrasting fabric 7 cm x 16 cm (2¾ in x 6¼ in) for the apron border. With right sides together, join the border to the apron along a 16 cm (6¼ in) edge. Hem three sides of the apron, leaving the top edge unhemmed. Sew a length of lace trim all round the three hemmed apron edges.

24. Run a gathering thread along the top raw edge of the apron piece. Pull up the gathers slightly to measure 10 cm (4 in) across. Cut a 72 cm x 5 cm (28½ in x 2 in) piece of white fabric for the waistband.

Matching the centres of the waistband and gathered edge of the apron, bind the apron waist edge, forming tie ends at each side.

25. *To make the hat*, transfer the pattern on page 73 on to tracing paper and cut out. Pin the traced pattern to the white fabric and cut four pieces. Cut four hat pieces from vilene two left pieces and two right pieces. Iron the vilene to the fabric hat pieces.

26. With right sides together, join the hat pieces together from point A to point B to form the centre seam. Turn one hat right side out and slip it inside the other hat, with right sides together and matching the seams. Sew round the lower edge, leaving a gap in the seam as indicated on the pattern. Clip into the curves and turn through. Sew the gap in the seam closed.

27. Fold up the side 'wings' of the hat and, working from the inside of the hat, catch in place with a few stitches at each side. Stuff the top point of the hat well, and the crown lightly. Pull the hat on to the head, to the neck at the back, and pin in place. Stitch from ear level, round the forehead, to the other ear level.

28. *To make the hair*, cut sixty 60 cm (23⅝ in) lengths of wool. Tie them together tightly at the centre. Sew this centre to the centre of the forehead at the edge of the hat. Catch the hair to the face at each side, where the 'wings' of the hat start. Make a plait at each side and with a length of ribbon tie a bow round each plait. Wind another length of wool thirty times around three fingers and tie through the centre of the loops to form a bunch. Sew this bunch to the centre of the forehead to make the fringe.

29. *For the face*, cut a 5 cm (2 in) diameter circle of flesh-coloured fabric for the nose, and two eyes from black felt. Run a gathering thread round the outer edge of the circle, put a ball of stuffing into the centre, pull up the gathers tightly and sew off securely. Sew or glue the nose to the face. Glue on the eyes, and mark the eyelashes with a black waterproof felt-tipped pen. Using three strands of red embroidery cotton, embroider the mouth. Rouge the cheeks.

30. Transfer the tulip and leaf patterns on to tracing paper and cut out. Pin the traced patterns to the felt and cut out three tulips from the red felt and four leaves from the green felt. Glue these to the apron.

31. Dress the doll.

Fig. 5 Full-size face

Prima ballerina doll

Aspiring ballerinas will love this doll. She can be posed in different positions and her big feet make her even more endearing. She is 105 cm (42 in) tall.

1. **To make the body and arms**, transfer the patterns on pages 74 and 75 on to tracing paper and cut out. Pin the patterns to the flesh-coloured fabric and cut out two bodies on the fold and four arms.

2. With right sides together sew the arm pieces to the body pieces matching points A and B as indicated on the pattern. With right sides together, join the body pieces together, leaving a gap in the seam at the waist edge. Clip into all the corners and turn through.

3. Stuff the arms lightly. Topstitch across the tops of the arms at the shoulders, then across the arms at the position indicated on the pattern, to make 'elbows'.

4. Stuff the rest of the body, paying special attention to the neck area. Sew the gap in the seam closed, tucking in more stuffing if necessary.

5. Tie strong thread around the arms to form wrists, and sew in the ends neatly.

6. **To make the body bottom**, cut two pieces of fancy fabric each measuring 52 cm x 17 cm (20½ in x 6¾ in). With right sides together, join the 17 cm (6¾ in) edges to form a tube. Turn under a 1 cm (⅜ in) hem along one raw edge and sew in place. (*See* fig. 1.)

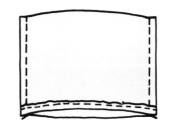

Fig. 1

7. **To make the legs**, transfer the legs pattern on page 75 on to tracing paper and cut out. Pin the traced pattern to the white T-shirting material and cut out four leg pieces.

8. With right sides together, join the legs in pairs round the outer edge, leaving the top edge open. Clip into the curves and turn through. Stuff the legs to the mark indicated on the pattern and stitch across each leg at this mark to make 'knees'. Continue stuffing the legs, but leave the top 3 cm (1¼ in) unstuffed.

9. Sew the tops of the legs closed, close to the raw edge. Sew the legs into the bottom seam of the body bottom as shown in fig. 2. Stuff the body bottom.

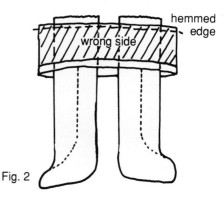

Fig. 2

10. Slip the body bottom over the body top and pin in place, 2.5 cm (1 in) below the underarms. Tuck in more stuffing if necessary. Sew the body bottom to the body top neatly all the way round, as shown in fig. 3.

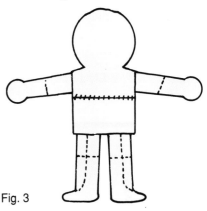

Fig. 3

11. **To make the shoes**, transfer the patterns on page 74 on to tracing paper and cut out. Cut two shoe uppers from plain fabric, two soles from cardboard and two soles from felt.

12. With right sides together join the back seams of the shoe uppers. Bind the inside edge of the shoe uppers with bias binding. Cut 8 mm (⅜ in) slits all the way round the bottom edge of the shoe uppers. Glue the cardboard soles to the inside of the shoe uppers by folding the fabric over the cardboard soles, as shown in fig. 4

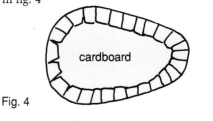

Fig. 4

13. Trim 2 mm (1/10 in) off all round the felt soles and glue them neatly over the underside of the shoes.

14. Push the feet into the shoes, matching the centre back seams of the legs and the shoes, and pin in place. Tuck in small amounts of stuffing to fill the gaps in the shoes. Sew the shoes neatly to the feet.

15. Cut two 1 m (1 yd 3 in) lengths of 15 mm (¾ in) wide ribbon and pin the centre of the ribbon to the top of the centre back seam of each shoe. Sew securely in place. Bring the ribbon ends to the front of the legs, cross over, take to the back of the legs, cross over and bring to the front of the legs again. Tie the ribbons in a bow at the front and catch them in place with a few stitches. Decorate the front of the shoes with sequins.

16. *To make the bodice,* transfer the bodice pattern on page 74 on to tracing paper and cut out. Pin the traced pattern to the fancy fabric and cut out two bodice pieces.

17. Decorate one of the bodice pieces (the front) with sequins. With right sides together, join the side seams. Bind the neck and armhole edges with bias binding. Sew a 25 cm (9⅞ in) length of 25 mm (1 in) wide ribbon to the inside of each shoulder section.

18. *To make the tutu,* join the short edges of each tulle layer to form eight separate circles. Turn them all right side out and slip them inside each other, matching all of the seams.

19. Run a gathering thread through all eight layers, along one raw edge. Pull up the gathers evenly, to fit round the bodice bottom. With right sides together, slip the bodice into the tulle tutu, and pin and tack in position as shown in fig. 5. Sew the tutu to the bodice and remove the tacking and gathering threads.

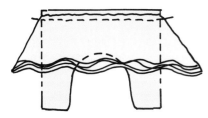

Fig. 5

20. Sew a flower and a ribbon bow to the one side of the waist seam. Glue sequins, at irregular intervals, to the different layers of tulle.

21. *To make the hair,* wind the wool around three fingers 20 times. Cut the wool from the ball. Tie a length of wool through the centre of the loops to form a curl. Make approximately twenty of these curls and sew them around the face, 3 cm (1¼ in) from the head seam. Trim any untidy ends.

Fig. 6

22. To cover the rest of the head, cut thirty-six 1 m (1 yd 3 in) lengths of wool. Tie a knot at one end of the bunch and divide the strands into three sections and plait them together. Tie a knot at the end of the plait. Starting at the centre front of the head, sew the plait around the head, just behind the curls.

23. Make more plaits and continue sewing them in a spiral pattern to the head, until the entire head is covered. Four plaits should be enough to cover the head. Cover any untidy joins left between the plaits with small artificial flowers and/or bows.

24. Sew an artificial flower to a length of 25 mm (1 in) ribbon and tie it in a bow round one upper arm. Tie a length of 15 mm (¾ in) ribbon round the neck and make a bow in front.

25. Cut the facial features from felt and glue them in place on the face. Mark the eyelashes on the doll's face with a black waterproof felt-tipped pen and, using three strands of red embroidery cotton, embroider the mouth.

26. Dress the doll and tie the shoulder ribbons together.

Fig. 7 Full-size face

Topsy-turvy Cinderella doll

Little girls will love turning Cinders into the Belle of the Ball. There are no pattern pieces for this doll – only measured pieces. She measures 50 cm (19 ¾ in) from the top of her head to the hem of her skirt.

going across the 11 cm (4⅜ in) edge. With right sides together, sew the arms as shown in fig. 2. Trim excess fabric from the corners and turn through.

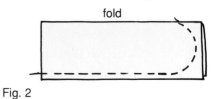

Fig. 2

REQUIREMENTS

46 cm x 50 cm (18⅛ in) of fabric, such as stockinette or T-shirting with the most stretch going across the 50 cm (19¾ in) edge for the heads, bodies and arms
Strong thread
Polyester filling
40 cm x 35 cm (15¾ in x 14 in) of white fabric for Cinders' blouse
1.4 m x 35 cm (55⅛ in x 14 in) of fancy fabric for the Cinderella ball gown
Lace trim for ball gown sleeves and neck edge
Bias binding for Cinders' blouse sleeve edges and neck
2 small buttons
Fabric off-cuts for the patches
Embroidery cotton in contrasting colours
1 m x 34 cm (1 yd 3 in x 13½ in) of blue fabric for Cinders' underskirt
1 m x 34 cm (1 yd 3 in x 13½ in) of black fabric for Cinders' overskirt
50 cm (19¾ in) of 13 mm (½ in) wide binding or ribbon to match each skirt
Ribbons, sequins etc. for decorating the Cinderella ball gown, and hair styles
Red embroidery cotton
Scraps of black and pink felt
Black waterproof felt-tipped pen
Glue
1 silver sequin
Wool for the hair – approximately 100 g (3½ oz)

1. *To make the doll's body*, cut a 28 cm x 46 cm (11 in x 18⅛ in) piece of flesh-coloured stockinette with the most stretch going across the 28 cm (11 in) edge. With right sides of the fabric together, join the long edges to form a tube. Turn through. Run a strong gathering thread round one raw edge of the tube, pull up the gathers tightly and sew off securely.

2. Stuff the tube so that it measures approximately 35 cm (14 in) round. Run a gathering thread round the other raw edge, pull up the gathers tightly and sew off securely.

3. *To form the heads*, measure 16 cm (6¼ in) from each gathered end and tie strong thread around the body tube at these levels. Don't tie too tightly or the heads will wobble (*see* fig. 1.).

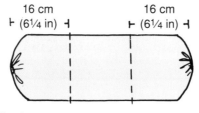

Fig. 1

4. *To make the bodices*, cut a bodice piece for each dress – one in white and one in fancy fabric – each measuring 35 cm x 8 cm (14 in x 3⅛ in). With right sides together, join the bodices together along one long edge. With right sides together, join the short edges together. Turn through.

5. Slip the bodice tube on to the body, matching the back seams. Pin in place round the waist seam. Run a gathering thread round each neck edge. Pull up the gathers to fit snugly round the necks and sew off. Adjust the gathers evenly round the necks.

6. *To make the arms*, cut two sleeves from each of the bodice fabrics, each measuring 16 cm x 17 cm (6¼ in x 6¾ in). With right sides together, join the short edges to form tubes. Run a gathering thread round one raw edge of each sleeve. Pull up the gathers tightly and sew off. Turn through.

7. From the stockinette fabric cut four arms each measuring 11 cm x 19 cm (4⅜ in x 7½ in), with the most stretch

8. Stuff the arms leaving the top 5 cm (2 in) unstuffed. With the seam in the centre, turn in the raw edges and oversew them closed.

9. Turn in a 5 mm (¼ in) hem on each sleeve and tack in place. Slip a sleeve over each arm, matching the seams, and sew the sleeves to the arms, around the bottom edges of the sleeves, 4.5 cm (1¾ in) from each hand edge.

10. Sew a length of lace trim round each ball gown sleeve. Sew a length of bias binding round each white sleeve. Sew the arms to the body at the shoulder positions, about 1.5 cm (¾ in) from the neck at each side. Sew a length of lace trim round the neck of the ball gown. Sew a length of bias binding round the neck of Cinders' bodice. Sew two buttons to the front of Cinders' bodice.

11. Cut two patches measuring 3 cm x 2 cm (1¼ in x ¾ in) and sew one to the sleeve and one to the bodice of the white top, using contrasting coloured embroidery cotton, and using large, uneven length stitches.

12. *To make Cinders' skirt*, cut a piece of blue fabric measuring 1 m x 34 cm (1 yd 3 in x 13½ in). Cut a piece of black fabric the same size. Cut one long edge of the black fabric into uneven points.

13. Pin the black fabric, right side up, on to the right side of the blue fabric and stitch together around the points and the straight edges using a zig-zag stitch. Cut out patches of various coloured fabric, in different sizes and sew them to the black section of the skirt using contrasting coloured embroidery cotton, using large, uneven stitches.

14. *To make the ball gown skirt*, cut a piece of fancy fabric measuring 1 m x 34 cm (1 yd 3 in x 13½ in). Decorate the skirt with lace and ribbons.

15. With right sides together, join the short edges of each skirt piece. Sew a length of lace trim to the ball gown skirt as shown in fig. 3. With right sides together, slip one of the skirt tubes into the other, matching the centre back seams. Sew the two skirt tubes together round the lower edge, being careful not to catch the ball gown's lace trim in the seam. Turn through.

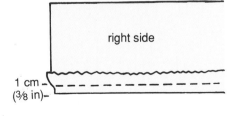

right side

1 cm
(3⁄8 in)

Fig. 3

16. Run a gathering thread round the waist edge of each skirt, separately. Pull up the gathers slightly and slip the skirts around the waist, matching the skirts to the bodices and the centre back seams. Pull up the gathers and adjust them to fit evenly round the waist of the doll. Sew the two skirts securely to the waist of the doll, turning the doll over to do the second skirt.

Fig. 4

fingers twenty times, cut off the wool and tie a piece of wool through the centre of the bunch, to form a curl. Sew this curl to the centre of the forehead to form a fringe.

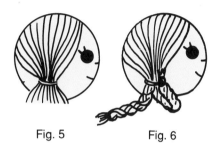

Fig. 5   Fig. 6

21. *To make the Belle of the Ball's hair*, cut ninety 1 m (1 yd 3 in) lengths of wool. Continue in the same way as for Cinders' hair to the stage of sewing the bunches of hair to the face at each side. Divide the hair at each side into two equal bunches and make two plaits at each side. Tie each plait securely with a piece of wool and trim the ends.

22. Take one plait at each side of the face, fold it in half and sew the tied end of the plait to the ear position, as shown in fig. 6. Take the other plait, at each side, wrap it around the folded plait at its base and catch it in place with a few stitches as you wrap. Tuck in the ends of the plaits neatly and sew in place. Make a fringe as for Cinders' hair, and decorate the hair with ribbon bows.

17. Sew 13 mm (½ in) wide binding or ribbon around each waist to cover the stitching lines. The binding or ribbon used for this should match the colour of each skirt.

18. Embroider the mouths and noses with red embroidery cotton. Cut the eyes from black felt and the cheeks from pink felt, and glue them in position. Mark the eyelashes with a black waterproof felt-tipped pen. Glue a silver sequin under one of Cinders' eyes.

19. *To make Cinders' hair*, cut ninety 66 cm (26 in) lengths of wool. Lay the hair across the head, spreading it out from the forehead, down the back of the head. Sew the hair to the head, along the centre, as shown in fig. 4.

20. Drape the hair down the sides of the head and catch it in place with a few stitches at each ear level, as shown in fig. 5. Make a plait at each side and tie a bow around each one, using different coloured ribbon. Wrap wool around two

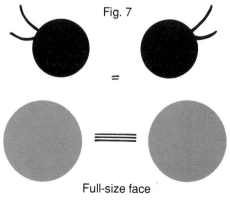

Fig. 7

Full-size face

White-faced clown

Older children and teenagers will enjoy having this very decorative clown in their bedrooms. You can decorate him very extravagantly and use rich, shiny fabrics for his costume.
He is 80 cm (31 ½ in) tall.

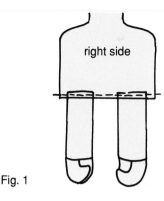

Fig. 1

1. *To make the legs and shoes,* cut two legs from the white T-shirting, each 32 cm x 17 cm (12⅝ in x 6¾ in) with the most stretch going along the 17 cm (6¾ in) edge. Transfer the shoe pattern on page 76 on to tracing paper and cut out. Pin the traced pattern to the fabric and cut out four pieces.

2. With right sides together, join the shoe pieces in pairs along the centre front seams. Clip into the curves and open the shoes out so that they lie flat. With right sides together, sew the top edge of the shoe pieces to the bottom edge of the legs.

3. Fold both of the legs in half lengthwise, with right sides together, and sew the back seam and the rest of the shoe seam. Turn through. Stuff each leg firmly, leaving the top 5 cm (2 in) unstuffed. Turn in

the raw edges at the top of each leg and oversew them closed, with the centre back and front seams centred.

4. *To make the head and body,* transfer the patterns on page 76 on to tracing paper and cut out. Pin the traced patterns to the white T-shirting and cut out two head and two body pieces.

5. With right sides together, join the head pieces round the outer edge, leaving the top edge open. Clip into the curves, turn through and stuff.

6. Run a gathering thread round the top edge of the head. Pull up the gathers tightly, tucking in more stuffing if necessary. Sew off securely.

7. With right sides together, sew the body side seams together. Clip into the curves and turn through.

8. Fold under a 1 cm (⅜ in) hem all round the bottom edge, and tack in place. Slip the tops of the legs into the body bottom and pin in position. Topstitch across the bottom edge of the body, sewing the tops of the legs into the seam as shown in fig. 1., and remove the tacking thread.

9. Stuff the body firmly. Turn in a 1 cm (⅜ in) hem around the neck edge and tack in position.

10. Insert the neck part of the head well into the neck of the body, tucking in more stuffing if necessary. Pin in position and sew neatly and securely in place. Remove the tacking thread.

11. *To make the arms,* transfer the pattern on page 76 on to tracing paper and cut out. Pin the traced pattern to the flesh-coloured fabric and cut out two arm pieces on the fold.

12. With right sides together, sew the underarm seams. Clip into the curves, turn through and stuff, leaving the top 5 cm (2 in) of the arm unstuffed.

13. With the seam to the centre, turn in and oversew the top raw edges, pulling up the stitches tightly to gather the tops of the arms slightly. Sew the arms to the body at shoulder position.

14. *To make the costume,* cut two bodice pieces each measuring 24 cm x 24 cm (9½ in x 9½ in). With right sides together, make the shoulder seams by sewing 2 cm (¾ in) across from the armhole edge on each side as shown in fig. 2.

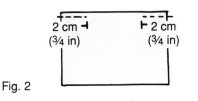

Fig. 2

15. Cut two sleeves, each measuring 20 cm x 26 cm (7⅞ in x 10¾ in). Run a gathering thread along one 26 cm (10¾ in) edge. Pull up the gathers to measure 18 cm (7 in) across, with most of the gathers in the centre.

16. With right sides together, pin the sleeve to the armhole edge of the bodice, matching the centre of the sleeve to the shoulder seam. Sew the sleeves in place.

17. With right sides together, join the underarm and side seams.

18. Hem the wrist edges of the sleeves. Measure a length of elastic to fit snugly round the wrist. Using a zig-zag stitch, and stretching the elastic as you sew, sew the elastic to the inside of the wrist hem, overlapping the ends of the elastic.

19. *To make the pantaloons,* cut two pieces of fabric each 31 cm x 44 cm (12¼ in x 17⅜ in). With right sides together, sew them together as shown in fig. 3. The 4 cm (1½ in) seams will be the centre back and centre front seams.

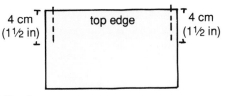

Fig. 3

20. Run a gathering thread along each top edge separately, from seam to seam. With right sides together, pin the centre front and centre back seams of the pantaloons to the centre front and centre back of the bodice piece.

21. Pull up the gathers on each side to fit the bodice. Pin in place and then sew the whole way around, thus attaching the pantaloons to the bodice.

22. With right sides together, join the inside leg seam, sewing a V-shape at the crotch area. Clip into the curves and turn through.

23. Hem the lower edges of the pantaloon legs. Measure two lengths of elastic to fit snugly round the legs. Using a zig-zag stitch, and stretching the elastic as you sew, sew the elastic to the inside of the pantaloons hem, overlapping the ends of the elastic. Place the costume on the clown body.

24. Turn in a 1 cm (⅜ in) hem round the neck and run a gathering thread around it. Pull up the gathers to fit snugly round the neck and sew the neck of the costume to the neck of the doll.

25. Decorate the costume with sequins and ribbon bows.

26. *To make the hat,* transfer the pattern on page 76 on to tracing paper and cut out. Pin the traced pattern to the fabric and cut out two hat pieces. Cut two hat pieces from the iron-on vilene.

27. Iron a vilene piece to the wrong side of each hat piece.

28. With right sides together, join the hat pieces around the outer edge leaving the bottom edge open. Turn in an 8 mm (⅜ in) hem around the bottom edge and sew in place.

29. Turn the hat right side out, stuff it and pin it in position on the head. Sew it neatly in place.

30. *To make the face,* cut a 6 cm (2⅓ in) diameter circle of white T-shirting for the nose. Run a gathering thread round the outer edge. Put a ball of stuffing into the centre, pull up the gathers tightly and sew off securely. Glue or sew the nose to the face.

31. Using sequins, felt, fake gems etc., glue on a decorative face, embroidering the outline of the eyes with black embroidery cotton.

32. *To make the hair,* wrap the wool 20 times around two fingers. Tie a length of wool through the centre of the loops to form a bunch of curls. Sew this bunch to the centre of the forehead, at the base of the hat, to make a fringe.

33. Make more curls in this way, by wrapping the wool around four fingers instead of two. Sew these curls, starting at the sides of the head, in front of the side seam, and around the back of the head.

34. Decorate the shoes with sequins or braid. Make bows from the 6 mm (¼ in) ribbon and glue one to the front of each shoe. Sew a bell to the front of each shoe.

35. Using the 2 cm (¾ in) wide ribbon, tie a bow around the neck.

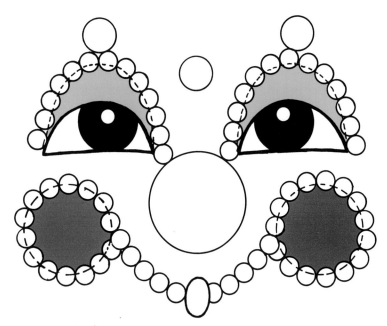

Fig. 4 Full-size face

Fancy dress bunny

This toy looks like a little child dressed up as a bunny for a fancy dress party. It carries a tiny bunny in the pocket and is 55 cm (21 ⅝ in) high, excluding the ears.

REQUIREMENTS
48 cm x 24 cm (19 in x 9½ in) flesh-coloured fabric for the face and hands
1 m x 85 cm (1 yd 3 in x 33½ in) white fake fur fabric for the body, ears, feet, tail and pocket
19 cm x 26 cm (7½ in x 10¾ in) pink fabric for the ear linings
Polyester stuffing
Red and black embroidery cotton
Glue
Scraps of black, white, pink, red and grey felt
Black waterproof felt-tipped pen
Scrap of brown fake fur or wool for the fringe
1 m (1 yd 3 in) of 25 mm (1 in) wide ribbon
Scrap of 6 mm (¼ in) wide ribbon

1. *To make the head*, transfer the face and head patterns on page 77 on to tracing paper and cut out. Pin the traced patterns to the fabrics and cut out two face pieces from flesh-coloured fabric and one head back and two head fronts from the fake fur fabric.

2. With wrong sides together, tack together the two face pieces around the outer edge.

3. With right sides together, join the two head front pieces along the centre seam, above and below the face opening.

4. Turn in 1 cm (⅜ in) around the face opening edge of the bunny and tack in place. Lay the head front piece, right side up, centrally over the face piece and pin it in position.

5. Sew the face in place, and remove the tacking thread.

6. Trace the mouth and the whiskers lightly on to the face. Embroider the mouth using three strands of red embroidery cotton. Embroider the whiskers, using two strands of black embroidery cotton.

7. *To make the ears*, transfer the pattern on page 77 on to tracing paper and cut out. Pin the traced pattern to the fabric and cut out two ear pieces in fake fur fabric and two ear pieces in the lining fabric. Trim 5 mm (¼ in) around the outer edge of the lining pieces, excluding the lower edge.

8. With right sides together join the fur ears to the lining ears in pairs, easing the fur pieces to fit, leaving the bottom edge open. Turn through.

9. Fold the base of the ears as indicated on the pattern and tack across the folds. Pin and tack the ears to the head front in the positions indicated on the pattern, lining side down as shown in fig. 1.

Fig. 1

10. With right sides together, sew the head back to the head front, leaving the neck edge open, incorporating the ears into the seam. Turn through and stuff.

11. Run a gathering thread round the neck edge, pull up the gathers tightly and sew off securely.

12. *To make the nose*, cut an 8 cm (3⅛ in) diameter circle from the flesh-coloured fabric. Run a gathering thread around the outer edge, put a ball of stuffing into the centre, pull up the gathers tightly and sew off securely. Glue or sew the nose to the face. Glue a black felt triangle on to the nose. Glue on black felt eyes, white felt eye 'sparkles', pink cheeks and a red mouth. Mark the eyelashes with the black waterproof felt-tipped pen.

13. Glue a scrap of brown fake fur or sew a few curls of brown wool to the centre of the forehead to make a fringe.

14. *To make the body*, transfer the body and hand patterns on page 78 on to tracing paper and cut out. Pin the traced body pattern to the fake fur fabric and cut out two pieces. Pin the hand pattern to the flesh-coloured fabric and cut out four pieces.

15. With right sides together, sew a hand piece to each arm at the wrist edge. With right sides together, sew the body back to the body front, leaving the neck and the ankle edges open.

16. Clip into the curves and turn through. Stuff the arms and then topstitch across them at the armholes. Topstitch across the tops of the legs as indicated on the pattern. Stuff the legs.

17. Run a gathering thread round the ankle edges, pull up the gathers tightly and sew off securely.

18. Stuff the rest of the bunny body. Run the gathering thread round the neck edge, pull up the gathers tightly and sew off securely.

19. *To make the feet*, cut two 16 cm (6¼ in) diameter circles from the fake fur fabric. Run a gathering thread round the outer edge and pull up the gathers slightly. Fill the centre with stuffing, pull up the gathers tightly, tucking in more stuffing if necessary. Sew off securely.

20. Pin the feet to the ends of the legs and sew neatly in place.

21. *To make the tail*, use a 20 cm (7⅞ in) diameter circle of fake fur fabric. Run a gathering thread round the outer edge and pull up the gathers slightly. Fill the centre with stuffing, pull up the gathers tightly, tucking in more stuffing if necessary. Sew off securely. Sew the tail to the lower back of the body.

22. *To make the pocket*, transfer the pattern on page 78 on to tracing paper and cut out. Pin the traced pattern to the fake fur fabric and cut out one pocket.

23. Turn in and sew a small hem all the way round the pocket piece. Pin the pocket to the centre of the bunny's tummy and sew in place.

24. Position the head on top of the body. Ladder stitch the head to the body, sewing around the neck a few times, to make it very secure. Tie the 25 mm (1 in) wide ribbon round the neck in a bow.

25. *To make the baby bunny*, transfer the patterns on page 78 on to tracing paper and cut out. Pin the traced patterns to the felt and cut two bodies and two ears from grey felt, two ear linings from pink felt, one snout from white felt, and one nose from black felt.

26. Glue an ear lining to each ear and slip the ears between the two body pieces at the positions indicated on the pattern. Sew the body pieces together, leaving the bottom edge open and incorporating the ears into the seam.

27. Stuff the body lightly and oversew the bottom edges together.

28. Glue on the snout and the nose. Embroider the eyes and the whiskers. Embroider the mouth. Make a small bow from 6 mm (¼ in) wide ribbon and glue it in position on the baby bunny's neck.

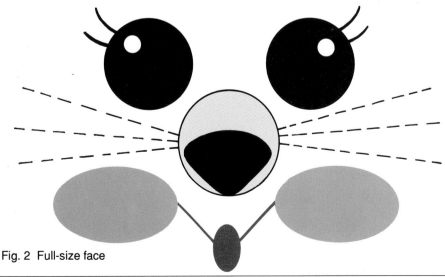

Fig. 2 Full-size face

Parachute puppy lampshade

This is a real conversation piece for a child's room.
Choose colours to match the decor.

REQUIREMENTS

40 cm (15¾ in) diameter frame
Fabric for the shade 52 cm x 38 cm
  (20½ in x 15 cm) of each of three
  colours
Fabric off-cuts for the body and ears
Strong thread
Glue
Polyester filling
1 m (1 yd 3 in) of 25 mm (1 in) wide
  ribbon in each of three colours for
  the bows
1.5 m (60 in) of 8 mm (⅜ in) wide
  ribbon for suspending the puppy
1.8 m (70¾ in) of narrow cord for
  threading through the cover
Ribbon for the puppy's neck
1 small bell
Scraps of black and red felt
Black embroidery cotton
1 pair of 18 mm (¾ in) diameter
  wobbly eyes
2 small beads
1 large bead
Off-cuts of white fabric for the
  clouds
75 cm (29½ in) of 8 mm (⅜ in) wide
  ribbon for suspending the clouds

1. *To cover the lampshade*, measure around the widest part of the frame (this one measures 137 cm (54 in) round). There are nine panels, so divide the measurement, in this case 137 cm by 9, to get the width of each panel. Add 2 cm (¾ in) to the width for the seam allowances, therefore for this lampshade each panel must measure 17.2 cm (6¾ in) across. Measure the height of the frame from the top to the bottom along one of the metal supports and add 5 cm (2 in) to this measurement for the hems. This frame measures 33 cm (13 in), so the panels must be 38 cm (15 in) long.

2. Cut three panels from each of the three colours of fabric. Alternating the colours, and using 1 cm (⅜ in) seams, join the panels to form a tube.

3. Fold under 5 mm (¼ in) then 8 mm (⅜ in) again, along one raw edge for the top of the cover. Sew this hem in place, leaving a small gap in the seam for threading through the cord. Hem the lower edge of the tube by turning under 5 mm (¼ in) and then 1 cm (⅜ in), also leaving a gap in the seam for threading through the cord.

4. Using a large blunt needle or hairclip, thread the narrow cord through the gap in the hem on the upper edge. Slip the cover over the frame, pull up the cord ends, adjusting the gathers evenly, to fit the top of the frame. Tie the ends of the cord together tightly and trim off the excess ends. Using some strong thread, catch the lampshade cover to the top of the frame, all the way round.

5. Thread the cord through the lower edge hem in the same manner. Pull up the cord ends tightly, adjusting the gathers evenly and tie the ends. Trim off the excess ends.

6. *To make the puppy*, transfer the patterns on page 78 on to tracing paper and cut out. Pin the traced patterns to the fabric and cut two body pieces and four ear pieces.

7. With right sides together, join the ears in pairs, leaving the straight edges open. Clip into the curves and turn through. Tack the ears to the right side of one of the body pieces in the position indicated on the pattern, as shown in fig. 1.

Fig. 1

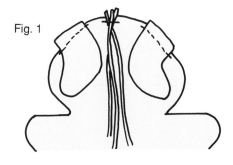

8. Cut three 50 cm (19¾ in) lengths of 8 mm (⅜ in) wide ribbon and tack them to the centre of the head between the ears as shown in fig. 1.

9. With right sides together, join the body pieces together, leaving a gap in the seam as indicated on the pattern, thus incorporating the ears and the suspending ribbons into the seam. Clip into the curves and turn through.

10. Stuff the arms first, then topstitch across the shoulders as shown on the pattern. Stuff the head, the body and the legs. Sew the gap in the seam closed. Topstitch across the tops of the legs as indicated on the pattern.

11. Thread the bell on to the ribbon, and tie it around the puppy's neck with the knot at the back.

12. Using two strands of black embroidery cotton, embroider the mouth. Cut the tongue from red felt and the nose from black felt and glue them in position. Glue on the wobbly eyes.

13. Tie the suspending ribbons together with a knot 1.5 cm (¾ in) from the head. Thread all three ribbons through the small, then the large, then the other small bead. Stitch the ends of the ribbons securely to the centre of three panels of the same colour, checking that the puppy hangs straight.

14. *To make the clouds*, transfer the patterns on page 79 on to tracing paper and cut out. Pin the traced patterns to a double layer of white fabric and cut three clouds from each pattern.

15. With right sides together, join the cloud pieces in pairs, sewing a length of ribbon into the seam, and leaving a gap in the seam. Vary the lengths of the ribbon and sew them into different positions on the clouds, to hang unevenly. Clip into the curves and turn through.

16. Stuff the clouds and sew the gaps in the seams closed. Sew the ends of the ribbons to the centre of the remaining panels, alternating shapes and levels.

17. Make three bows from each of the three different coloured 25 mm (1 in) wide ribbons and glue them over the ends of the suspending ribbons to hide the stitching, alternating the colours.

Carousel lampshade

Make this for someone special. The carousel would look equally lovely made in primary colours.

REQUIREMENTS
40 cm (15¾ in) diameter lamp-shade frame
Fabric to cover the shade:
 52 cm x 38 cm (20½ in x 15 in) of each of three colours
Strong cotton
18 bells
2 m (2¼ yd) of 8 mm (⅜ in) wide ribbon to match each of the three fabric colours
Felt in three colours for the horses:
 40 cm x 42 cm (15¾ in x 16½ in) of each colour
Scraps of black felt
Wool in three colours for the horses' tails
1 m (1 yd 3 in) of 15 mm (¾ in) wide ribbon in each of three col-ours to match the narrow ribbon
Glue
Polyester stuffing
Sequins and braid to decorate the horses
1.8 m (70¾ in) of narrow cord for threading through the cover

1. *To cover the lampshade* (*see* instructions for the Parachute Puppy Lampshade on page 32).

2. *To make the horses*, transfer the horse patterns on page 79 on to tracing paper and cut out. Pin the traced patterns to the felt and cut out three pairs of body pieces, three pairs of ears, three saddles and three manes in each of the three colours. This will give you nine horses. Cut the eyes from black felt.

3. Cut short slits into each of the horse mane felt pieces as indicated on the mane pattern.

4. Tack a mane to the wrong side of one body piece of each horse as indicated on the pattern. Cut a 40 cm (15¾ in) length of the 8 mm (⅜ in) wide ribbon for each horse and glue in place to the wrong side of the body piece, as shown in fig. 1. Leave 10 cm (4 in) of ribbon hanging from under the tummy of each horse.

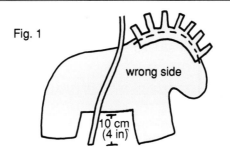

Fig. 1

wrong side

10 cm (4 in)

5. With right sides facing out, sew the pairs of body pieces together, leaving a gap in the seam along the back, as indicated on the pattern. Trim the outer edge of the horses to neaten. Stuff the bodies and sew the gap in the seams closed.

6. Trim the manes shorter at the front.

7. Fold the bottom edge of each ear in half and glue the fold together. Glue the ears to the heads in the positions indicated on the pattern.

8. *To make a tail*, cut fifteen 15 cm (6 in) lengths of wool. Cut one 16 cm (6¼ in) length of wool and use it to tie the lengths together in the middle. Sew the tail to the horse at the position indicated on the pattern, through the tie in the middle. Tie a length of wool tightly around the tail, just below the base, to form it into a neat bunch. Trim the tail ends neatly.

9. Glue on the saddles over the back seam, and the eyes in the positions indicated on the pattern.

10. Make three small bows from each of the three different coloured 8 mm (⅜ in) wide ribbons. Alternating the colours, glue the bows to the centre front of the horses' necks.

11. Decorate the horses with braid trim and sequins.

12. Trim the ribbons hanging from under the tummies to different lengths and sew a bell to the end of each.

13. Thread a bell on to each of the upper suspending ribbons and knot them in place, approximately 3 cm (1¼ in) up from the horses' backs.

14. Pin the suspending ribbon ends to the lampshade at each seam between the pa-nels. Trim the ribbons so that the horses hang at different levels.

15. Make three bows from each of the three different coloured 15 mm (¾ in) wide ribbons. Glue these bows over the stitches attaching the suspending rib-bons to the lampshade, alternating the colour sequence.

Sleepy time teddies

Wearing their cute bunny slippers and pyjamas, these teddies are ready for bed. They are 55 cm (21 ⅝ in) tall.

REQUIREMENTS
(FOR EACH TEDDY)

56 cm x 36 cm (22 in x 14¼ in) of fake fur fabric for the head, ears and hands
12 cm x 16 cm (4¾ in x 6¼ in) piece of fabric for ear linings
1 pair of 20 mm (¾ in) diameter safety eyes
1 safety nose, 1 cm (⅜ in) across
Black embroidery cotton
110 cm x 45 cm (43⅓ in x 17¾ in) of fabric for the body
Polyester filling
2x 10 cm (4 in) diameter circles of white fake fur fabric for the bunny slippers
Scrap of pink felt
2 pink beads
4 black beads
Glue
Ribbon to tie around the neck
2 buttons

1. *To make the ears*, transfer the pattern on page 80 on to tracing paper and cut out. Pin the traced pattern to the fur fabric and cut two ear pieces. Pin the same traced pattern to the ear lining fabric and cut two pieces.

2. With right sides together, sew an ear lining to each fur fabric ear, leaving the straight edge open. Turn through.

3. *To make the head*, transfer the patterns on page 80 on to tracing paper and cut out. Pin the patterns to the fur fabric and cut one snout, one head front on the fold, and two head back pieces, remembering to reverse the pattern for a left and a right side.

4. With right sides together, join the centre back seam. Sew the darts in the front piece, at the upper and the lower edges as indicated on the pattern. Matching the large dots shown on the pattern, sew the snout piece to the head front from point X to point X. Join the seam from the neck edge to the snout tip.

5. Pin the ears, lining side down, to the right side of the head front at the position indicated on the pattern. Sew the head back to the head front, easing the front and stretching the head back slightly to fit, thus incorporating the ears into the seam. Turn through.

6. Insert the safety nose and eyes on the head front. Stuff the head firmly. Run a gathering thread round the neck edge. Pull up the gathers tightly and sew off securely, tucking more filling into the neck if necessary.

7. Using six strands of black embroidery cotton, embroider the mouth as illustrated in fig. 1.

Fig. 1

8. *To make the body*, transfer the patterns on pages 80 and 81 on to tracing paper and cut out. Pin the traced patterns to the body fabric and cut out two body pieces on the fold, one pocket piece on the fold, four leg pieces and two soles. Pin the hand pattern to the fake fur fabric and cut out four hand pieces.

9. With right sides together, sew a hand piece to each wrist edge.

10. To make the back pocket, cut a 24 cm x 5 cm (9½ in x 2 in) piece of body fabric for the pocket binding. Gather the pocket piece across the upper edge. Pull up the gathers to measure 23 cm (9¼ in) across. Bind this edge. Gather the lower edge of the pocket piece to fit the lower edge of the body piece. With right sides facing up, pin and tack the pocket piece to one of the body pieces, ensuring that the bound edge of the pocket is on a level with the underarms.

11. *To make the legs*, join the leg pieces, right sides together, along the centre back and front seams. Clip into the curves. Cut little slits around the lower edges of each foot. With right sides together, pin and sew the soles to the lower edges of the feet. Turn through and stuff the legs to within 2 cm (¾ in) of the top edge. Bring the centre back and front seams together in the centre and tack across the raw edges to hold them together.

12. Tack the legs to the body front piece as shown in fig. 2. With right sides together, sew the body pieces together around the outer edge, leaving the neck edge open. Clip into the corners and turn through. Sew two buttons to the centre front. Stuff the arms and topstitch across the armholes. Stuff the body.

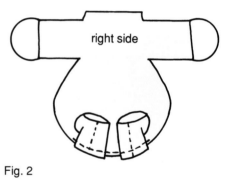

right side

Fig. 2

13. Turn in a 1 cm (⅜ in) hem round the neck edge and run a gathering thread round it. Pull up the gathers, tucking in more filling. Sew off securely. Stitch the head centrally and securely to the body.

14. *To make the bunny slippers*, run a gathering thread round the outer edges of the white fur circles. Put a ball of stuffing into the centre and pull up the gathers tightly, adding more stuffing if necessary to make a nice round shape. Sew off securely. Sew on a pink bead for the nose and two black beads for the eyes. Cut out four ears from pink felt and glue on to the head of the bunny. Glue the bunnies to the top of each foot.

15. Tie a bow around the teddy's neck.

Sleepy bunny pyjama bag

Pyjamas are stored in the pillow while the little bunny takes a nap. The bunny makes a cute toy on its own too.

REQUIREMENTS

25 cm (9⅞ in) of white fake fur fabric for the bunny

18 cm x 20 cm (7 in x 7⅞ in) of pink fabric for the ear linings

2 pieces of fabric for the mattress, each measuring 55 cm x 32 cm (21⅝ in x 12⅝ in)

44 cm x 30 cm (17⅜ in x 12 in) of quilted fabric for the blanket

3 pieces of fabric for the pillow, each measuring 30 cm x 24 cm (12 in x 9½ in)

Polyester stuffing

Strong thread

1 safety nose, 1 cm (⅜ in) across

Black embroidery cotton

45 cm (17¾ in) of 5 cm (2 in) wide anglaise trim

45 cm (17¾ in) of bias binding

25 cm (9⅞ in) of lace trim for the pillow

1 m (1 yd 3 in) of 24 mm (1 in) wide ribbon.

---

1. *To make the bunny*, transfer the patterns on page 82 on to tracing paper and cut out. Pin the traced patterns to the fake fur fabric and cut out two head pieces, two ears, one head gusset and two body pieces. Mark the dart lines on one (under) body piece. Cut two ears from the pink lining fabric.

2. With right sides together, fold the underbody in half lengthwise, and sew the curved dart seam. Trim excess fabric from the dart seam.

3. With right sides together, join the two body pieces around the outer edge, leaving a gap in the seam, for stuffing, as indicated on the pattern.

4. Clip into the curves, and turn through. Stuff the body firmly and sew the gap in the seam closed.

5. *To make the tail*, cut a 16 cm (6¼ in) diameter circle of fake fur fabric. Run a gathering thread round the outer edge.

Put a ball of stuffing into the centre and pull up the gathers tightly. Sew off securely. Sew the tail to the body upper at the rear end.

6. *To make the head*: with right sides together sew the head gusset to one of the head pieces from point X to point Y. With right sides together sew the gusseted head piece to the other head piece round the entire outer edge, leaving the neck edge open.

7. Clip into the curves and turn through. Insert the safety nose at the point of the gusset. Stuff the head firmly. Run a gathering thread round the neck edge, pull up the gathers tightly, tucking in more stuffing, and sew off securely.

8. *To make the ears*: with right sides together, join the ear linings to the fake fur ears, leaving the bottom edge open. Turn through.

9. Turn in a small hem round the raw edge and oversew the edges together. Pin the ears in position on the head and sew neatly and securely to the head. Catch the back of the ears to the head with a few stitches, so that they stand away from the head slightly.

10. Embroider the closed eyes, in a V-shape, with black embroidery cotton.

11. Sew the head securely to the body, between the front paws, with the face turned to one side. Tie a bow around the neck with the ribbon.

12. *To make the bed*, cut the blanket piece as shown in fig. 1.

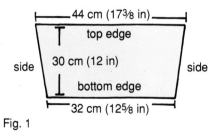

Fig. 1

13. Sew the lace trim to the top edge of the blanket and bind with bias binding.

14. Pin the blanket, right side up to the right side of one mattress piece and tack in place, as shown in fig. 2.

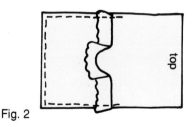

Fig. 2

15. With right sides of the fabric together, sew the two mattress pieces together, leaving a gap in the seam at the top for inserting stuffing. Turn through and stuff the mattress, not too firmly. Sew the gap left in the seam closed and even-out the matress' stuffing.

16. Sew a length of lace trim to one of the pillow pieces. Hem one of the 30 cm (12 in) edges by turning under 5 mm (¼ in) then 8 mm (⅜ in) and sewing it in place forming the top edge of the bunny's pillow. See fig. 3. This will form the pillow pocket.

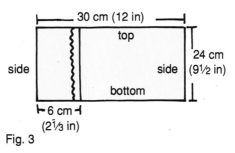

Fig. 3

17. Pin the pocket piece, wrong side down, to the right side of one of the other pillow pieces. Tack it in place, leaving the top hemmed edge free.

18. With right sides together, sew the third pillow piece to the tacked-together pillow and pocket round the edges, leaving a gap in the bottom edge seam. Be careful not to catch the hemmed edge of the pocket into the seam. Turn through and stuff. Sew the gap in the seam closed.

19. Mark a line 20 cm (7⅞ in) from the top edge of the mattress. Stitch the bottom edge of the pillow to the mattress along this line.

20. Tuck the bunny under the blanket with front paws and head on the pillow.

Man-in-the-Moon pillowcase

*Children will love sleeping on a moon and stars pillowcase.
The Man-in-the-Moon is nice to hold while falling asleep.
Make the pillowcase in colours to match the bedroom.*

REQUIREMENTS
2 pieces of fabric each measuring
  75 cm x 50 cm (29½ in x 19¾ in)
  for the pillowcase
Fabric off-cut for the moon pocket
  33 cm x 48 cm (13 in x 19 in)
Felt pieces for the stars
14 cm x 12 cm (5½ in x 4¾ in) flesh-
  coloured felt for the head and body
Red T-shirting off-cut for the suit
Strong thread
Polyester filling
1 small bell
Red and black embroidery cotton
Scrap of ribbon for the neck

1. Hem one short edge of each pillowcase piece by turning under 1 cm (⅜ in) then 4 cm (1½ in).

2. *To make the moon pocket*, transfer the pattern on page 83 on to tracing paper and cut out. Pin the traced pattern to a double layer of fabric and cut out.

3. With right sides together, sew round the outer edge, leaving a gap in the seam as indicated on the pattern. Clip into the curve and turn through. Sew the gap in the seam closed.

4. Topstitch all the way round the outer edge, 5 mm (¼ in) from the edge. Pin the moon in position on one of the pillowcase pieces and sew in place, leaving the upper edge free.

5. *To make the stars*, transfer the pattern on page 83 on to tracing paper and cut out. Pin the traced star pattern to the felt and cut out four yellow stars and two white stars.

6. Pin the stars in position on the front pillowcase piece and sew in place.

7. With right sides together, join the two pillowcase pieces together round the three raw edges, leaving the hemmed edges open. Turn through.

8. *To make the Man-in-the-Moon's head and body*, cut a piece of flesh coloured felt measuring 14 cm x 12 cm (5½ in x 4¾ in). Join the short edges. Turn

through. Run a gathering thread round one raw edge. Pull up the gathers tightly and sew off securely.

9. Stuff the tube firmly. Centre the seam and oversew the raw edges. Make the neck by tying strong thread tightly around the tube, 6 cm (2⅓ in) from the bottom edge.

10. *To make the suit*, transfer the pattern on page 83 on to tracing paper and cut out. Pin the traced pattern to the red T-shirting and cut out two suit pieces.

11. *To make the hood*, cut a piece of red T-shirting fabric measuring 6 cm x 14 cm (2⅓ in x 5½ in) with the most stretch going across the 14 cm (5½ in) edge. Turn in and sew a tiny hem along one 14 cm (5½ in) edge.

12. With right sides together, fold the hood piece in half and sew a slightly curved seam, as shown in fig. 1. Turn through. Pull the hood on to the head and sew neatly around the face edge. Wrap strong thread round the neck to hold the hood in place.

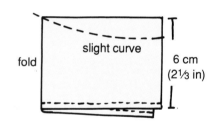

fold
slight curve
6 cm (2⅓ in)

Fig. 1

13. With right sides together, join the suit pieces round the outer edge, leaving the neck edge open as indicated on the pattern. Clip into the curves; turn through.

14. Stuff the legs and the arms lightly. Pull the suit over the body, up to neck level. Turn in a small hem around the neck edge of the suit and sew to the body, pulling up the stitches to fit snugly. Tie the ribbon in a bow round the neck.

15. *To make the hands and the feet*, tie strong thread around each arm and leg, 2 cm (¾ in) from each edge. Sew in the ends of the thread neatly.

16. Embroider the eyes, nose and mouth, and sew a bell to the hood.

Paddy the draught stopper

This friendly leprechaun keeps out draughts in winter. In summer he hangs from the doorknob.

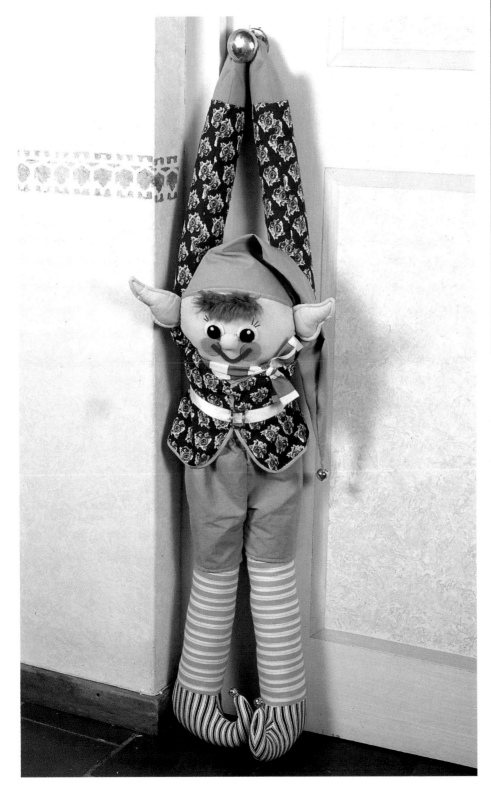

REQUIREMENTS

- 1 m x 50 cm (1 yd 3 in x 19¾ in) of flesh-coloured fabric for the body, head, arms and ears
- 45 cm x 52 cm (17¾ in x 20½ in) of striped fabric for the legs
- 48 cm x 28 cm (19 in x 11 in) of fabric for the shoes
- 34 cm x 24 cm (13½ in x 9½ in) of fabric for the hands
- 28 cm x 72 cm (11 in x 28¼ in) of fabric for the shorts
- 60 cm x 70 cm (23⅝ in x 28 in) of fabric for the jacket
- 1.5 m (60 in) of bias binding
- 60 cm x 56 cm (23⅝ in x 22 in) of fabric for the hat
- 66 cm x 10 cm (26 in x 4 in) of fabric for the scarf
- Polyester stuffing
- Strong thread
- 3 bells
- 48 cm (19 in) of 25 mm (1 in) wide tape or ribbon for the belt
- 1 buckle
- Small scrap of brown fake fur
- Scraps of white, black, red and pink felt
- Black waterproof felt-tipped pen
- Glue
- Short length of 8 mm (⅜ in) elastic for the shorts' waist

1. ***To make the ears***, transfer the pattern on page 84 on to tracing paper and cut out. Pin the traced pattern to the flesh-coloured fabric and cut two pairs of ears.

2. With right sides together, join the ears together in pairs, using an 8 mm (⅜ in) seam, leaving the head edge open. Clip into the curves and turn through.

3. Stuff the ears and topstitch all the way round, 8 mm (⅜ in) from the edge.

4. ***To make the body and head***, transfer the pattern on page 84 on to tracing paper and cut out. Pin the traced pattern to the flesh-coloured fabric and cut out two body pieces, marking the dart lines.

5. With right sides together, fold the body pieces to match the dart lines. Sew along the dart lines. Trim excess fabric from the dart seam.

6. Pin and tack the ears to the right side of one body piece, in the position indicated on the pattern, as shown in fig. 1. (*See* next page.)

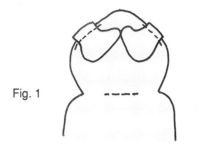

Fig. 1

7. With right sides together, join the body back and front, leaving a gap in the bottom seam as indicated on the pattern. Clip into the curves and turn through. Stuff the body firmly and sew the gap in the seam closed.

8. *To make the arms*, cut two pieces from the flesh-coloured fabric, each measuring 44 cm x 21 cm (17⅜ in x 8½ in). With right sides together, join the long edges together.

9. Turn the arms right side out. Centre the seam and turn in a 1 cm (⅜ in) hem at one raw edge. Oversew this edge, pulling up the stitches tightly to gather slightly.

10. Stuff the arms, not too firmly. Run a gathering thread round the raw (wrist) edge, pull up the gathers tightly and sew off securely.

11. *To make the hands*, transfer the pattern on page 84 on to tracing paper and cut out. Pin the traced pattern to the fabric and cut out four hand pieces.

12. With right sides together, join the hand pieces in pairs, leaving the wrist edges open. Clip into the curves and turn through. Stuff the hands.

13. Turn in a 1 cm (⅜ in) hem round the wrist edge and tack in position. Pull the hands over the wrist ends of the arms, matching the seam at the thumb side of the hand to the seam in the arm.

14. Sew the arms to the body with the seams of the arms facing the body.

15. *To make the shoes and legs*, transfer the shoe pattern on page 85 on to tracing paper and cut out. Pin the traced pattern to the fabric and cut out four shoe pieces.

Cut two legs, each measuring 45 cm x 26 cm (17¾ in x 10¾ in), from the striped fabric.

16. With right sides together, join the shoe pieces in pairs along the centre front, to the point indicated on the pattern. Open out the shoes and, with right sides together, sew a shoe to each leg.

17. With right sides together, sew the centre back leg seam, and the rest of the shoe seam together. Clip into the curves and turn through.

18. Stuff the legs firmly, leaving the top 12 cm (4¾ in) of the legs unstuffed. Turn in and tack a 1 cm (⅜ in) hem around the raw edge of each leg. Matching the back seams, oversew the two legs together as shown in fig. 2.

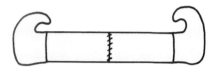

Fig. 2

19. Using strong thread, tie tightly around this joining seam. Sew the legs, at this tied section, to the centre of the body bottom seam.

20. *To make the shorts*, transfer the pattern on page 84 on to tracing paper, and cut out. Pin the traced pattern to the fabric and cut out two shorts pieces on the fold.

21. With right sides together, join the centre seams. Bring the centre seams together, to the middle, and sew the inside leg seam. Clip into the curves and turn through.

22. Turn in and hem the lower edges of the shorts neatly.

23. At the waist edge, turn in 5 mm (¼ in) and then 8 mm (⅜ in). Sew this hem in place, leaving a gap in the seam for threading the elastic.

24. Measure a length of elastic to fit snugly around the waist plus 1 cm (⅜ in). Thread the elastic through the gap in the seam, overlap the elastic ends by 5 mm (¼ in), and sew them together securely. Sew the gap in the seam closed.

25. Adjust the gathers evenly around the waist. Place the shorts on the body.

26. *To make the jacket*, transfer the pattern on page 85 on to tracing paper, and cut out. Pin the traced pattern to the fabric and cut out two jacket fronts, one jacket back on the fold, and two sleeves, each measuring 40 cm x 22.5 cm (15¾ in x 8¾ in).

27. With right sides together, join the back and fronts at the shoulders.

28. Open the jacket out and, with right sides together, sew on the sleeves as shown in fig. 3., matching the centre points of the individual sleeves with the shoulder seams.

29. With right sides together, join the side and underarm sleeve seams. Clip into the curves and turn through.

30. Bind the entire outer edge of the jacket with bias binding.

31. Turn in a 1 cm (⅜ in) hem at the wrist edges of the sleeves, and tack in place. Place the jacket on the body.

32. Overlap the jacket fronts and catch them together, along the centre front edge, from the neck edge to half way down the front.

33. Sew the sleeves to the hands at the wrist edges.

34. Bring the hands together, and sew the fingertips together.

35. *To make the hat*, cut two hat pieces as shown in fig. 4.

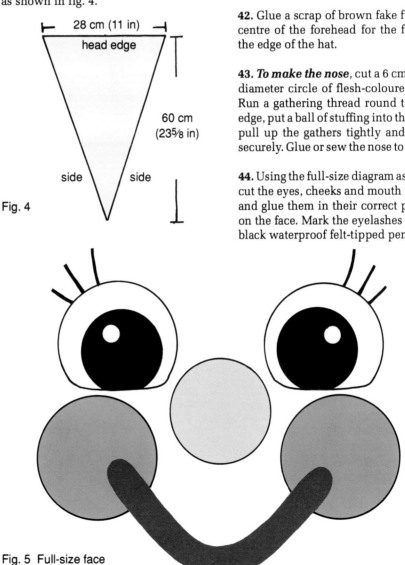

Fig. 4

36. With right sides together, join the side seams. Turn through. Turn in a 1 cm (⅜ in) hem round the raw edge and sew in place.

37. Pin the hat to the head and sew neatly in place, all round the head edge.

38. Sew one of the bells to the point of the hat.

39. *To make the belt*, measure the tape or ribbon to fit round the waist, over the bulk of the jacket. Fit the belt round the waist, turning under the ends, and overlapping and sewing them together. Sew the buckle to the centre front of the belt.

40. Tie the unhemmed scarf piece around the neck, with the knot positioned to one side.

41. Sew a bell to the point of each shoe.

42. Glue a scrap of brown fake fur to the centre of the forehead for the fringe, at the edge of the hat.

43. *To make the nose*, cut a 6 cm (2⅓ in) diameter circle of flesh-coloured fabric. Run a gathering thread round the outer edge, put a ball of stuffing into the centre, pull up the gathers tightly and sew off securely. Glue or sew the nose to the face.

44. Using the full-size diagram as a guide, cut the eyes, cheeks and mouth from felt and glue them in their correct positions on the face. Mark the eyelashes with the black waterproof felt-tipped pen.

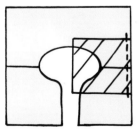

Fig. 3

Fig. 5 Full-size face

Clown doorstop

This clown doorstop prevents doors from banging, at the same time adding colour and interest to a bedroom.
He stands 52 cm (20½ in) tall.

1. *To cover the cardboard base,* run a gathering thread round the outer edge of the fabric circle, lay the cardboard circle in the centre of the fabric one, on the wrong side. Pull up the gathers tightly to fully enclose the cardboard circle and sew off securely.

2. *To make the body and the head,* cut the stockinette and the two contrasting body fabrics as shown in fig. 1.

3. With right sides together, join the two contrasting body pieces along one 32 cm (12⅝ in) edge. With right sides together, join the head piece to the body piece along the 67 cm (26½ in) edge. With right sides together join the two sides to make a tube.

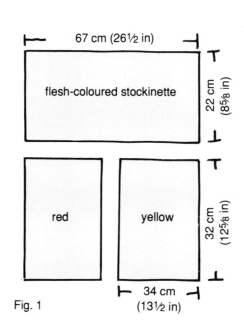

67 cm (26½ in)

flesh-coloured stockinette

22 cm (8⅝ in)

red   yellow

32 cm (12⅝ in)

34 cm (13½ in)

Fig. 1

4. Turn in and sew a 1 cm (⅜ in) hem along the lower edge of the body. Sew the body tube all the way around the lower edge, to the covered base.

5. Place a layer of stuffing into the base of the tube, then put in the weight. Complete stuffing the body and the head.

6. Run a gathering thread round the top edge of the head. Pull up the gathers tightly, tucking in more stuffing if necessary. Sew off the gathering thread securely. Run a gathering thread around the join between the head and the body. Pull up the gathers to form a neck, and sew off securely.

7. *To make the hat,* transfer the pattern on page 83 on to tracing paper and cut out. Pin the traced pattern to the fabric and cut out one pair of hat pieces from each of the two fabrics.

8. With right sides together, join the contrasting pairs of hat pieces along the centre seam. With right sides together, join the hat back and front round the outer edge, leaving the lower edge open. Clip into the curves and turn through.

Fig. 3 Full-size face

9. Turn in and sew a 1 cm (⅜ in) hem around the lower edge of the hat. Sew the ric-rac braid around the hem. Stuff the points of the hat relatively firmly, and the crown lightly.

10. Pin the hat to the head, tucking in more stuffing where necessary. Sew the hat neatly to the head.

11. *To make the arms and hands*, cut one arm piece in each contrasting fabric, each measuring 18 cm x 20 cm (7 in x 7⅞ in). Cut two hand pieces from stockinette, each measuring 20 cm x 7 cm (7⅞ in x 2¾ in), with the most stretch along the 20 cm (7⅞ in) edge.

12. With right sides together, sew a hand piece to each arm piece along the 20 cm (7⅞ in) edge. With right sides together, join the underarm seam of each sleeve, sewing as shown in fig. 2. Trim excess fabric and turn through.

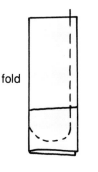

fold

Fig. 2

13. Stuff the arms. Turn in 1 cm (⅜ in) at the raw edges. Run a gathering thread round the top of each arm, pull up the gathers tightly and sew off securely.

14. Sew the arms securely to the body at shoulder level, contrasting the arms to the body at each side.

15. *To make the neck frill:* with right sides together join the short edges of the fabric. Hem one raw edge. Turn in 5 mm (¼ in) along the other raw edge and run a gathering thread around it.

16. Slip the neck frill over the head, pull up the gathers tightly and sew securely to the neck.

17. *To make the hair*, wind the wool around two fingers 12 times, cut off the wool and tie another piece of wool

through the centre of the loops to form a curl. Make more curls and sew them around the base of the hat, from ear to ear to form the fringe. Make the rest of the hair in the same way, but wind the wool around four fingers to make longer curls. Sew the curls from ear to ear round the back of the hat.

18. *To make the nose*, run a gathering thread round the edge of the red fabric circle. Place a ball of stuffing into the centre, pull up the gathers and sew off securely. Glue or sew the nose to the face.

19. Cut the eyes, eye 'sparkles', mouth and cheeks from felt and glue in position. Mark the eye-lines with the black waterproof felt-tipped pen.

20. Glue the 6 mm (¼ in) wide ribbon around the base, and the wrists. Make three small bows from the length of ribbon and glue one to the centre front of the ribbon around the base. Glue one bow to each wrist.

21. Sew a bell to each hat point. Glue the two pompons on the centre front seam.

Hen and chickens doorstop

This mother hen and her chicks is the ideal doorstop for the kitchen.

1. *To make the base*, transfer the pattern on page 87 on to tracing paper and cut out. Draw a line around the traced pattern on to the cardboard and cut out one cardboard base. Pin the same traced pattern to the calico and cut out one base, adding 4 cm (1½ in) all the way round.

2. Run a gathering thread round the edge of the calico. Place the cardboard base in the centre. Pull up the gathers to enclose the cardboard, and sew off securely

3. *To make the body and the head*, transfer the patterns on page 86 on to tracing paper and cut out. Pin the body pattern to the calico and cut two pieces. Pin the head pattern to the brown fabric and cut two pieces. Pin the beak pattern to the orange fabric and cut two pieces.

4. *To make the hen's comb and the wattles*, transfer the patterns on page 86 on to tracing paper and cut out. Pin the traced patterns to the red fabric off-cuts and cut out two comb pieces and four wattle pieces.

5. With right sides together, join the comb pieces and the wattle pieces in pairs round the outer edges, leaving the bottom edges open. Clip into the curves and turn through.

6. Stuff the comb and the wattles lightly. Sew the open edges closed.

7. Pin and tack the comb and one wattle to the right side of one of the head pieces as shown in fig. 1.

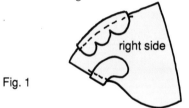
Fig. 1

right side

8. Tack the other wattle to the right side of the other head piece.

9. With right sides together, sew a beak piece to each head piece at the position indicated on the pattern, incorporating the wattles into the seam.

10. *To make the wings*, cut four pieces from the fabric, each measuring 22 cm x 15 cm (8⅝ in x 6 in). Round off the two bottom corners of each piece, as shown in fig. 2.

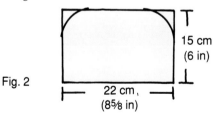
Fig. 2

15 cm (6 in)

22 cm (8⅝ in)

11. With right sides together, join the wings in pairs, leaving the long straight edge of each wing open. Turn through.

12. Run a gathering thread along the raw edges of each wing. Pull up the gathers to measure 8 cm (3⅛ in) across.

13. Pin and tack the wings to the body pieces as shown in fig. 3.

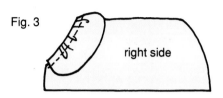
Fig. 3

right side

14. With right sides together, sew a head piece to each body piece, incorporating the wings into the seams.

15. *To make the tail*, transfer the patterns on pages 86 and 87 on to tracing paper and cut out. Pin the traced patterns to the fabrics and cut out one pair of each tail feather in black, brown and red.

16. With right sides together, join one set of tail feather pieces, and then join the second set.

17. With right sides together, join the two sets of tail feathers together, matching the seams as you go. Clip into the curves and turn through.

18. Stuff the tail and then topstitch round the feathers as shown in fig. 4.

Fig. 4

19. Tack the tail to the right side of one body piece at the position indicated on the pattern, as shown in fig. 5.

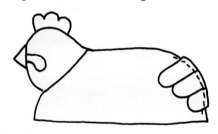
Fig. 5

20. With right sides together, join the body pieces round the outer edge, leaving the bottom edge open, thus incorporating the tail into the seam. Clip into the curves and turn through.

21. Turn under a 1 cm (⅜ in) hem around the bottom edge and stitch it in place.

Fig. 6 Full-size eye

22. Pin the body to the covered base along the bottom edge. Sew neatly in place, leaving a gap in the seam for stuffing as indicated on the pattern.

23. Stuff the hen firmly, pushing the weight into the centre of the body, and padding well all around it. Sew the gap in the seam closed, tucking in more stuffing as required.

24. From felt, cut two black eyes, two white eye 'sparkles', and two black nostrils. Glue them in place. Mark the eyelashes with a black waterproof felt-tipped pen.

25. Glue the black tape around the neck, over the seam, with the join of the tape at centre front.

26. Make a bow from the 20 mm (¾ in) wide ribbon and glue it over the black tape join.

27. Starting at the centre back of the body, stitch the 5 cm (2 in) wide brown ribbon to the bottom edge of the body all the way around, folding the ends of the ribbon over to make a neat join.

28. *To make the chicks*, transfer the patterns on page 87 on to tracing paper and cut out. Pin the traced patterns to the yellow felt and cut out six bodies and six wings. Cut three beaks and six feet from orange felt.

29. Sew the body pieces in pairs around the outer edge, incorporating a beak. Leave a gap in the seam.

30. Stuff the bodies firmly and sew the gap in the seam closed.

31. Glue on the wings, and the feet. Mark the eyes with the black waterproof felt-tipped pen.

32. Tuck the chicks into the ribbon.

Parrot mobile

Use your imagination and fabric off-cuts to create these wonderfully colourful birds. They brighten any room from the entrance hall to the kitchen.

REQUIREMENTS
Fabric off-cuts for the head, body, chest gusset, tail, beak and wings in the colours of your choice
Felt off-cuts to compliment the fabric colours used for the head feathers
50 cm (19¾ in) of broad ric-rac braid
One pair of 2.5 cm (1 in) diameter wobbly eyes
Ribbon pieces of various widths, lengths and colours for the tail feathers
1 large bell for the neck
Bells of different sizes for the tail
Polyester filling
Glue
Ribbon for the neck bow
Cord or ribbon for hanging at the desired height

1. *To make the beak*, transfer the pattern on page 88 on to tracing paper and cut out. Pin the traced pattern to the fabric and cut out two beak pieces. With right sides together, sew the beak pieces together round the outer edge, leaving the straight edge open for stuffing. Clip into the curves of the beak and turn through. Stuff the beak and sew the open edge closed. Topstitch along the line indicated on the pattern.

2. *To make the body*, transfer the patterns on page 88 on to tracing paper and cut out. Pin the traced patterns to the fabric and cut out two head pieces, two body pieces, one chest gusset, and two tail pieces.

3. With right sides together, sew a head piece to each body piece, matching point A and point B.

4. *To make the parrot's head plumes*, transfer the patterns on page 88 on to tracing paper and cut out. Pin the traced patterns to the felt and cut out one plume of each size.

5. Tack the head plumes, cord or ribbon for hanging the parrot and the beak to the right side of one of the head pieces as shown in fig. 1.

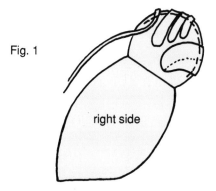

Fig. 1

right side

6. With right sides together, sew one side of the chest gusset to one of the body pieces, matching and sewing from point B to point C. With right sides together, join the two body pieces, sewing the free edge of the chest gusset to the second body piece, leaving the tail edge open. Clip into the curves and turn through.

7. Stuff the body. Turn in an 8 mm (⅜ in) hem round the tail edge and run a gathering thread around it. Pull up the gathers tightly, tucking in more filling if necessary, and sew off securely.

8. *To make the tail*, cut various widths and colours of ribbon in lengths varying from 17 cm (6¾ in) to 27 cm (10½ in). Use up to 15 ribbon pieces in all. Bring all the ends together at one side and sew them together. Tack the end of the ribbons to the right side of one of the tail pieces as shown in fig. 2.

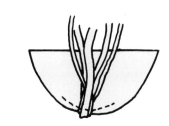

Fig. 2

9. With right sides together, sew the two tail pieces together, thus incorporating the ribbons into the seam, and leaving the straight edge open. Trim excess fabric and ribbon ends at the point. Turn through. Turn under a 1 cm (⅜ in) hem round the raw edge and tack in place. Stuff the tail.

10. Pin the parrot's tail to the body, over the gathered opening, and sew neatly in place.

11. *To make the wings*, transfer the patterns on page 89 on to tracing paper and cut out. Pin the traced main wing section pattern to the fabric and cut four pieces. Pin the traced outer wing feather patterns to the felt and cut two of each size.

12. With right sides together, join the main wing sections in pairs, leaving a gap in the seam as indicated on the pattern. Clip into the curves and turn through. Stuff the wings lightly and sew the gap in the seam closed. Pin the felt outer wing feathers to the main wings in the positions indicated on the pattern, remembering to make a left and a right wing. Topstitch as indicated on the pattern. Sew or glue the wings to the body.

13. Sew bells to the ends of the parrot's tail ribbons.

14. Glue the ric-rac braid round the neck seam and round the base of the tail where it joins the body. Thread the bell on to a length of ribbon. Tie the ribbon in a bow, incorporating the bell into the knot. Glue this bow to the centre front of the neck.

15. Cut two eye surrounds from felt and glue them in position. Glue the wobbly eyes to the eye surrounds.

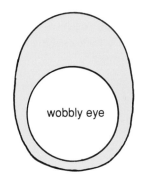

wobbly eye

Fig. 3 Full-size eye

Clown hoop mobile

This mobile can be hung against the wall or can swing freely from the ceiling. The tubing is obtainable from hardware shops.

REQUIREMENTS
96 cm (38¼ in) of 15 mm (¾ in) diameter clear plastic tubing
2.5 cm (1 in) of 12 mm (½ in) diameter wooden dowel rod
80 coloured beads to fit into the plastic tubing
Glue
1 large bell
90 cm (35½ in) of 24 mm (1 in) wide ribbon
50 cm (19¾ in) of 8 mm (⅜ in) wide ribbon
1 large and 2 small beads
Ribbon or cord for hanging the mobile
Polyester stuffing
36 cm x 23 cm (14¼ in x 9¼ in) of fabric for the clown's body and arms
10 cm x 16 cm (4 in x 6¼ in) of flesh-coloured fabric for the clown's head
Scrap of lace for the clown's neck frill
Ribbon for the neck bow
Felt scraps for the hat and facial features
2 small pompons
2 small bells
Black waterproof felt-tipped pen
Red embroidery cotton
Scraps of wool for the clown's hair

1. Push the dowel rod halfway into one end of the tubing. Fill the tubing with the beads to within 1.5 cm (¾ in) of the open end. Push the open end of the tubing over the other half of the dowel rod. Glue a piece of 24 mm (1 in) wide ribbon over the join, with the join of the ribbon positioned at the top.

2. Thread a large bell into the centre of a 50 cm (19¾ in) length of 8 mm (⅜ in) wide ribbon. Knot the ribbons together 4 cm (1½ in) from the bell, then thread both ribbon ends through a small, then large, then small bead. Knot the ribbon lengths together 5 cm (2 in) up from the last small bead.

3. Glue the two ends of this beaded ribbon round the ribbon covering the join of the tubing. Tie a length of ribbon or cord round the join for hanging the mobile, reinforcing the knot with glue. Make two bows from the 24 mm (1 in) wide ribbon and glue them on to the top of the plastic hoop to cover any untidy joins or knots.

4. *To make the clown*, transfer the patterns on page 89 on to tracing paper and cut out. Pin the traced patterns to the fabric and cut out two heads from flesh-coloured fabric, two arms on the fold and two body pieces on the fold from brightly coloured fabric.

5. With right sides together, sew a head piece to each body piece. Sew the arms as indicated on the pattern, and turn through. Stuff the arms lightly, leaving the bottom 6 cm (2⅓ in) at the hand ends unstuffed.

6. Tack the arms to the right side of one body piece in the position indicated on the pattern, as shown in fig. 1.

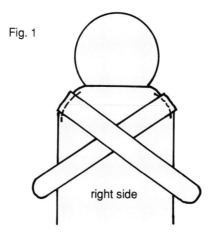
Fig. 1

right side

7. With right sides together, join the two body pieces, stitching as shown on the pattern and incorporating the ends of the arms into the seam, leaving the top of the head open. Cut through the centre of the legs to divide. Clip into all the corners and curves and turn through.

8. Stuff the legs and topstitch across the tops of the legs where they join the body. Stuff the body and the head. Sew the gap in the seam closed.

9. Glue a piece of lace round the neck with the join at the front. Make a tiny ribbon bow and glue it over the join.

10. *To make the hat*, transfer the pattern on page 89 on to tracing paper and cut out. Pin the traced pattern to the felt and cut out one hat piece.

11. Overlap and glue the straight edges together to form a cone shape. Stuff the hat lightly and glue it on to the head. Glue a pompon to the point of the hat.

12. Sew a few loops of wool to the centre of the forehead and at each ear position for the hair.

13. Cut a nose from red felt and two cheeks from pink felt and glue in position. Mark the eyes with the black waterproof felt-tipped pen. Using two strands of red embroidery cotton, embroider the mouth.

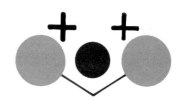
Fig. 2 Full-size face

14. Glue a small pompon to the centre front of the body. Sew a bell to each foot.

15. Fold the unstuffed hands around the bottom of the plastic hoop and catch the edge of the hands securely to the arms with a few stitches.

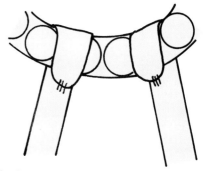
Fig. 3

Sociable scarecrow storage hanging

He's so friendly – not even the birds are scared of him. Store toys and pencils and crayons in nis pockets. He is 1 m (1 yd 3 in) tall.

REQUIREMENTS

62 cm x 60 cm (24½ in x 23⅝ in) of fabric for the shirt

22 cm x 52 cm (8⅝ in x 20½ in) flesh-coloured fabric for the head

Fabric off-cuts for the hands, patches, pockets, hat and shoes

Polyester stuffing

Strong thread

90 cm x 70 cm (35½ in x 28 in) of denim for the dungarees

Wool for the hair

60 cm (23⅝ in) of 15 mm (¾ in) diameter dowel rod

8 cm (3⅛ in) diameter red fabric circle for the nose

Scraps of black, white, red, pink and orange felt

Glue

Black waterproof felt-tipped pen

2 large buttons

Ribbon for the bow-tie

Short length of ribbon or cord for the hanging loop

Embroidery cottons for sewing on the patches.

1. To make the shirt, cut one back piece and one front piece as shown in fig.1. Turn under and sew a 1 cm (⅜ in) hem at each wrist edge. With wrong sides together, fold the back piece as shown in fig. 2. and sew a seam 3 cm (1¼ in) from the fold, to form a tube for the dowel rod on the right side.

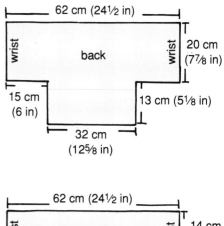

62 cm (24½ in)

wrist | back | wrist

20 cm (7⅞ in)

15 cm (6 in)

13 cm (5⅛ in)

32 cm (12⅝ in)

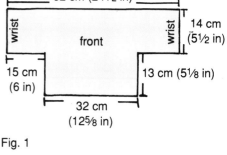

62 cm (24½ in)

wrist | front | wrist

14 cm (5½ in)

15 cm (6 in)

13 cm (5⅛ in)

32 cm (12⅝ in)

Fig. 1

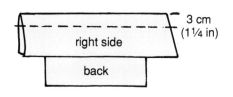

right side

back

3 cm
(1¼ in)

Fig. 2

2. *To make the head*, transfer the head pattern on page 90 on to tracing paper and cut out. Pin the traced pattern to the flesh-coloured fabric and cut two head backs. For the head front, cut out a 22 cm (8⅝ in) diameter circle from the same fabric. With right sides together, join the head back pieces from point A to point B at each side as indicated on the pattern. With right sides together, join the head back to the head front round the outer edge, leaving a gap in the seam, as indicated on the pattern, as shown in fig. 3. Clip into the curves and turn through.

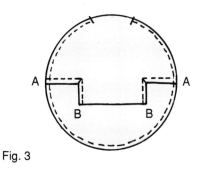

A   A

B   B

Fig. 3

3. Position the head centrally on the shirt back piece and tack in place, as shown in fig. 4. With right sides together sew the shirt back to the shirt front along the top edge, thus incorporating the head into the seam.

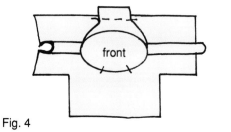

front

Fig. 4

4. Leaving the wrist edges open, and with right sides together, sew the shirt back to the shirt front around the outer edge from the lower wrist edge on one sleeve piece to the lower wrist edge on the other sleeve piece. Clip into the corners and turn through.

5. *To make the hands*, transfer the hand pattern on page 90 on to tracing paper and cut out. Pin the traced pattern to the fabric and cut out four hand pieces. With right sides together join the hand pieces in pairs, leaving the wrist edges open. Clip into the curves and turn through.

6. Stuff the hands. Run a gathering thread round the wrist edges, pull up the gathers tightly and sew off securely. Insert one hand into the wrist edge of one sleeve, thumb up, and sew the sleeve neatly to the hand, leaving the dowel tube free.

7. Stuff the shirt and sew the other hand into the other wrist edge in the same manner as the other hand.

8. Stuff the head and sew the gap in the seam closed. Catch the head to the shirt front with a few stitches behind the chin.

9. *To make the dungarees*, cut two pieces of denim as shown in fig. 5. From one short edge, measure and cut a slit 34 cm (13½ in) long, through both pieces of denim, to divide for the legs. On the dungaree front piece, sew a line 17 cm (6¾ in) down from the top edge, as shown in fig. 6.

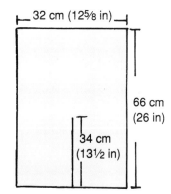

32 cm (12⅝ in)

66 cm
(26 in)

34 cm
(13½ in)

Fig. 5

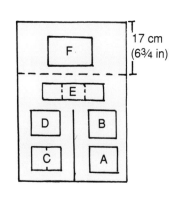

F

E

D   B

C   A

17 cm
(6¾ in)

Fig. 6

10. *To make the pockets*, cut six pockets as shown in fig. 7. Turn in and sew a 1 cm (⅜ in) hem along the top edge of each pocket. Turn in and tack a 1 cm (⅜ in) hem along the other three sides.

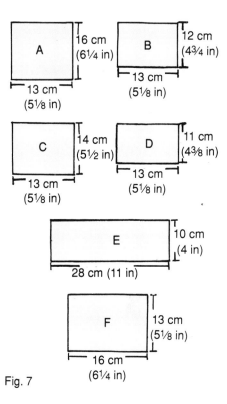

A

16 cm
(6¼ in)

13 cm
(5⅛ in)

B

12 cm
(4¾ in)

13 cm
(5⅛ in)

C

14 cm
(5½ in)

13 cm
(5⅛ in)

D

11 cm
(4⅜ in)

13 cm
(5⅛ in)

E

10 cm
(4 in)

28 cm (11 in)

F

13 cm
(5⅛ in)

16 cm
(6¼ in)

Fig. 7

11. Pin the pockets in position on the dungaree front as shown in fig. 6. Sew the pockets in place, reinforcing the stitching at each top edge. Sew along the centre of pocket C to divide it into two smaller pockets. Sew two seams on pocket E to divide it equally into three smaller pockets. Remove the tacking threads.

12. With right sides together, join the dungaree front to the dungaree back along the sides and the inner leg edges. Clip into the corners and turn through.

13. Topstitch through both layers along the line on the front, 17 cm (6¾ in) from the top edge. Turn in and sew a 1 cm (⅜ in) hem along the top edge. Hem the trousers by turning up 1 cm (⅜ in) then another 3 cm (1¼ in) to the right side, and sew in place.

14. *To make the shoes*, transfer the shoe patterns on page 90 on to tracing paper and cut out. Pin the traced patterns to the fabric and cut out four shoe pieces and two sole pieces. With right sides together, join the shoe pieces in pairs along the centre back and the centre front seams.

Make tiny slits all round the bottom raw edges. Pin the soles to the shoes, with right sides together, and matching X and Y points. Sew in place, clip into the curves and turn through.

15. Stuff the shoes, leaving the top 6 cm (2⅓ in) unstuffed. With the toes pointing to the front, insert the shoes into the trouser bottoms and pin in place. Stitch across the trouser bottoms, through all the layers, sewing close to the lower edge of the trouser turn up.

16. Cut two 5 cm (2 in) squares of fabric for the patches on the shoes and sew to the side of each shoe, using contrasting embroidery cotton and big, uneven stitches. Cut one 4.5 cm (1¾ in) square of fabric and sew it to the hand in the same manner as the shoe patches.

17. *To make the shoulder straps*, cut four pieces of denim, each measuring 9 cm x 34 cm (3½ in x 13½ in). With right sides together, join the straps in pairs round the outer edge, leaving one short edge open. Turn through and top-stitch the three seamed edges 5 mm (¼ in) from the edge. Sew the raw edges of the shoulder straps to the inside of the dungaree back, 1.5 cm (¾ in) in from the side seams, as shown in fig. 8.

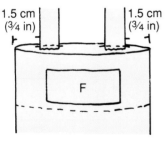

Fig. 8

18. *To make the hat*, cut a fabric piece measuring 40 cm x 14 cm (15¾ in x 5½ in) for the hat and another piece measuring 40 cm x 6 cm (15¾ in x 2⅓ in) for the turn-up. With right sides together, join the short edges of each piece to form two tubes. Turn under and sew a 1 cm (⅜ in) hem along one edge of the turn-up. Turn the hat tube right side out, and, with the right side of the turn-up tube facing the wrong side of the hat tube, slip the turn-up tube into the hat tube, keeping the raw edges of both tubes level. Sew the two tubes together.

19. Fold the turn-up to the right side of the hat and pin it in place. Stitch the turn-up to the hat, sewing around the centre of the turn-up to hold it in place.

20. Turn over a 5 mm (¼ in) hem along the raw edge of the hat, and run a gathering thread round it. Pull up the gathers tightly and sew off securely. Turn through. Place a little stuffing in the hat, position and pin it on to the head, and sew neatly in place.

21. *To make the hair*, wind wool around three fingers to make a fringe. Cut wool from the ball, and, sewing through the centre of the bunch, sew the fringe securely to the centre front of the hat at the lower edge. Make a bunch of curls at each side of the face in the same way by winding the wool around four spread-out fingers instead of three.

22. *To make the nose*, run a gathering thread round the red fabric circle. Put a ball of filling into the centre on the wrong side. Pull up the gathers tightly and sew off securely. Cut out the eyes, cheeks, mouth and eye 'sparkles' from the felt and glue to the head. Mark the eyelashes on the face with the black waterproof felt-tipped pen.

23. Push the measured length of dowel rod through the fabric tube at the back of the scarecrow's shirt. Pull the dungarees on to the body, to the underarm level. Bring the shoulder straps from the back to the front and sew each strap in position on the dungaree front. Sew a button to each strap.

24. Tie the ribbon in a bow and glue it in position under the chin. Sew a loop of cord or ribbon to the back of the head for hanging the scarecrow.

25. *To make the birds*, transfer the bird patterns on page 90 on to tracing paper and cut out. Pin the traced pattern of the bird body to a double layer of black felt and trace round it. Sew along this line, leaving a gap in the seam. Cut out the felt birds, close to the stitching. Stuff the birds lightly, and sew the gap in the seam closed. Cut a beak and feet for each bird from orange felt and glue in place. Cut two white eyes for each bird and glue in place. Glue or sew the birds to the scarecrow's arms.

Fig.9 Full-size face

Clown Clock

This decorative wall hanging is a fun way of teaching children how to tell the time. It measures 62 cm (24 ½ in) from the tip of the hat to the bottom of the collar.

REQUIREMENTS
2 pieces of white fabric each
  measuring 35 cm (14 in) square
36 cm x 55 cm (14¼ in x 21⅝ in) of
  patterned fabric
75 cm x 40 cm (29½ in x 15¾ in) of
  batting
1 large red button with a shank
  4 cm (1½ in) in diameter
Scraps of felt for the numbers, eyes
  and hands
2 small plastic rings to fit over the
  button shank
2 'male' and 12 'female' press stud
  halves
Glue
Red embroidery cotton
A loop of cord or a plastic ring

1. Trace the face lightly on to the right side of one of the white fabric squares. Cut out the eyes from felt and glue them in position.

2. Transfer the patterns for the numbers on page 91 on to tracing paper and cut out. Pin the traced patterns to the felt and cut out, alternating the colours in the number sequence.

3. Pin the numbers in their correct position to the clock face and sew or glue neatly in place.

4. **To make the hat and collar**, transfer the patterns on page 92 on to tracing paper and cut out. Pin the traced pattern to the patterned fabric and cut out two hat and two collar pieces.

5. With right sides together, sew the hat front to the clock face at the top, and the collar front to the clock face at the bottom. Iron the seams open.

6. Using the clock front piece as a pattern, lay it right side up on to the batting. Cut out the batting with a 2 cm (¾ in) border. Tack the clock front to the batting round the outer edge.

7. With right sides together, sew the remaining hat and collar pieces to the clock back piece. With right sides together, sew the clock front and back pieces together, leaving a gap in one side seam for turning through. Trim the excess batting, turn through, and sew the gap closed.

8. Embroider the mouth using red embroidery cotton, or, using a close zig-zag stitch. Topstitch all round, 5 mm (¼ in) from the edge. Topstitch across the seams joining the collar and hat to the face.

9. **To make the hands**, transfer the patterns on page 92 on to tracing paper and cut out. Pin the patterns to a double layer of felt and trace round them. Sew along these traced lines, leaving the short, straight bottom edges free. Cut out the hands, stuff them, and sew the ends closed.

10. Sew a small plastic ring to the bottom edge of each hand. Slip the rings over the shank of the button and sew the button to the clock face as shown in fig. 1.

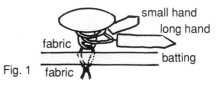

Fig. 1

11. Sew the 'male' half of a press stud to the underside of the small hand at its point. Using the press stud at the end of the small hand as a guide for the correct positioning, sew a 'female' half of a press stud on the clock face at each number. Use these studs as a guide for the correct positioning of the 'male' half of a press stud on the underside of the big hand.

12. Sew a loop of cord or a plastic ring at the back of the hat to hang the clock.

Toadstool toy bucket

Transform an ordinary plastic bucket into a delightful toy bucket. The frog is attached with velcro, so it can be removed. The toadstool then becomes a seat.

REQUIREMENTS

1 plastic bucket – the one illustrated is 26 cm (10¾ in) high and has a diameter of 26 cm (10¾ in)
1 m (1 yd 3 in) square of fabric to cover the bucket
40 cm (15¾ in) diameter circle of stiff cardboard.
48 cm (19 in) diameter circle of red fabric for covering the under-lid
54 cm (21¼ in) diameter circle of red fabric for the toadstool top
1 m (1 yd 3 in) of strong cord for threading through the cover
120 cm (47¼ in) of 15 mm (¾ in) wide tape
Polyester stuffing
Glue
Strong thread
5 cm (2 in) of velcro
Green fabric off-cuts for the frog's head
Green wool for the frog's arms and legs
White felt for the toadstool spots
36 cm x 22 cm (14¼ in x 8⅝ in) of fabric for the frog's body
1 pair of 2 cm (¾ in) diameter wobbly eyes
Felt scraps for the 'buttons'
Ribbon for the frog's bow
Felt off-cuts for the leaves and flowers

1. Remove the handle from the bucket.

2. **To cover the bucket,** measure it as shown in fig. 1. Add on 8 cm (3⅛ in) for the hem and this figure will indicate the diameter of the fabric circle required.

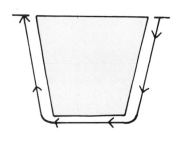

Fig. 1

3. Hem the edge of the circle, turning in 5 mm (¼ in) then 1 cm (⅜ in) and leaving a gap in the seam for threading through the cord.

4. Thread the cord through the gap in the hem. Place the bucket in the centre of the circle and pull the circle up and over the top of the bucket. Pull up the ends of the cord tightly and knot them together. Adjust the gathers evenly around the top of the bucket.

5. Place the cardboard circle on the wrong side of the 48 cm (19 in) red fabric circle. Fold over the excess fabric border, all the way round the cardboard circle, and glue in place on the cardboard.

6. Turn under a 1 cm (⅜ in) hem all the way round the 54 cm (21¼ in) red fabric circle, and pin and tack in place. Sew this circle to the covered cardboard base, around the edge, pleating the circle slightly to fit the base, and leaving a gap for stuffing.

7. Stuff the lid to an even toadstool shape. Sew the gap along the lid edge closed. Remove the tacking thread.

8. Position the lid centrally over the base and mark the positions for the tie-on's, at each side of the lid and at the corresponding points on the base.

9. Sew a 30 cm (12 in) length of tape to each of the four marked points. Tie the tapes together at each side, thus attaching the lid to the base.

10. From white felt, cut eight spots of various sizes and appliqué them to the toadstool lid.

11. **To make the frog's legs and arms,** cut thirty 45 cm (17¾ in) lengths of wool for each leg and thirty 28 cm (11 in) lengths of wool for each arm. Knot each bunch at one end. Plait each bunch and tie a knot at the end of each plait.

12. **To make the frog's body,** cut two pieces of fabric, each measuring 18cm x 22cm (7 in x 8⅝ in).

13. Pin and tack the arms and legs to the right side of one of the body pieces as shown in fig. 2.

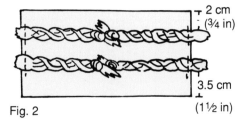

2 cm (¾ in)

3.5 cm (1½ in)

Fig. 2

14. With right sides together, join the body pieces along the side seams, incorporating the ends of the arms and legs into the seams.

15. Run a gathering thread around the bottom (leg) edge. Pull up the gathers and sew off securely. Turn through.

16. Stuff the body firmly. Run a gathering thread round the top (neck) edge. Pull up the gathers tightly, tucking in more stuffing if necessary, and sew off securely.

17. **To make the head,** cut a 21 cm (8¾ in) diameter circle from green fabric. Run a gathering thread around the outer edge. Put a ball of stuffing into the centre, pull up the gathers and sew off securely.

18. Make two eyeballs in a similar manner, using 9 cm (3½ in) diameter circles of green fabric.

19. Sew or glue the head to the body, between the arms, and with the gathered edge of the head to the body.

20. Sew or glue the eyeballs to the head, with the gathered edges to the head.

21. Glue the wobbly eyes to the eyeballs.

22. Make a bow from the ribbon and glue it to the centre front of the neck.

23. Cut out two small felt buttons and glue them to the centre front of the body.

24. Sew the velcro strip to the underside of the body and to the toadstool lid, with the soft half of the velcro on the lid.

25. Cut out flowers and leaves from felt, using the patterns on page 92. Glue them round the base of the toadstool.

Father Christmas wreath

Welcome guests over the festive season with this cheerful door decoration. The wreath measures 36 cm (14 ¼ in) in diameter.

REQUIREMENTS
1 wire coat hanger
110 cm x 21 cm (43⅓ in x 8(¾ in)
  of fabric for the wreath
Polyester stuffing
Strong thread
34 cm x 32 cm (13½ in x 12⅝ in) of
  red fabric for the hat and the body
32 cm x 15 cm (12⅝ in x 6 in) of
  flesh-coloured fabric for the hands
  and head
20 cm x 10 cm (7⅞ in x 4 in) of
  black felt, folded in half for the
  shoes
30 cm x 18 cm (12 in x 7 in) of white
  fake fur fabric for the beard and
  trim on the sleeves and hat
Glue
1 pair of 18 mm (¾ in) diameter
  wobbly eyes
Scrap of red felt
90 cm (35½ in) of 15 mm (¾ in)
  wide ribbon
2 large bells
1 m x 16 cm (1 yd 3 in x 6¼ in) of
  fabric for the large bow
13 cm x 8 cm (5⅛ in x 3⅛ in) of
  white fabric for the back of the
  head

1. *To make the wreath*: with right sides together, join the long edges of the wreath fabric to form a tube.

2. Turn through and stuff the tube.

3. Form the fabric tube into a circle and, turning in the raw edges, oversew the ends neatly together.

4. Pull the wire coat hanger into a circular shape to match the wreath.

5. Catch the coat hanger to the wreath, stitching all the way round, at the back of the wreath. (*See* fig. 1.)

6. *To make the Father Christmas*, transfer the patterns on page 93 on to tracing paper and cut out. Pin the traced patterns to the fabric and cut out two hat pieces

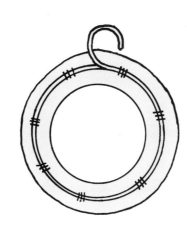

Fig. 1

and two body pieces from the red fabric; four hands and one head piece from the flesh-coloured fabric; one head piece from the white fabric. This will be the back of the head.

7. With right sides together, sew a hat piece to each head piece.

8. With right sides together, sew a head and hat piece to each body piece.

9. With right sides together, sew a hand piece to each side of the body back and front pieces.

10. With right sides together, join the two body pieces together, round the outer edge, leaving a gap in the seam as indicated on the pattern. Clip into the curves and turn through.

11. Stuff the body and sew the gap in the seam closed.

12. Transfer the beard pattern on page 93 on to tracing paper and cut out. Pin the traced pattern to the wrong side of the white fake fur fabric and cut out one beard piece.

13. Glue the beard, along the top edge, to the face in the position indicated on the pattern.

14. Cut a 25 cm (9⅞ in) length measuring 2 cm (¾ in) wide of white fake fur fabric. Glue the strip round the base of the hat, where it joins the head, overlapping the join at the back of the head.

15. Glue 2 cm (¾ in) wide strips of white fake fur fabric round the wrists, where the hands join the body.

16. Cut a nose from red felt and glue it on the face. Glue on the wobbly eyes.

17. Sew the Father Christmas to the wreath, catching him in place with a few stitches at the top of the hat and at each hand edge.

18. *To make the hat's pompon*, cut an 8 cm (3⅛ in) diameter circle of white fake fur fabric. Run a gathering thread round the outer edge. Put a ball of stuffing into the centre, pull up the gathers tightly and sew off securely.

19. Glue the white fur fabric pompon to the top of the hat.

20. Tie the 15 mm (¾ in) wide ribbon round the wreath, between the hands. Sew a large bell to each ribbon end.

21. *To make the shoes*, transfer the pattern on page 93 on to tracing paper and cut out. Pin the traced shoe pattern to a double layer of black felt and draw round the pattern.

22. Sew round the outline, leaving a gap in the seam as indicated on the pattern. Cut out the shoes, close to the stitching. Stuff the shoes and sew the gap in the seam closed.

23. Topstitch along the centre of the shoes as indicated on the pattern.

24. Glue the shoes to the body, between the arms.

25. *To make the large bow*, fold the bow fabric in half lengthwise and sew the three open edges together, leaving a gap in the centre of the seam along the long edge to turn through.

26. Turn through and sew the gap in the seam closed.

27. Using this fabric strip, tie a big bow. Glue or sew the bow to the wreath, below the shoes.

Gingerbread man Christmas tree ornament

Make these in plain or patterned fabric. You could join them at the hands and make a string of them to hang across your mantelpiece.

REQUIREMENTS
(FOR EACH GINGERBREAD MAN)

Fabric off-cuts for the body
White fabric scraps for the hands and feet
35 cm (14 in) of 8 mm (⅜ in) wide ribbon for the hanging loop and the neck bow
White ric-rac braid
Scraps of felt
Glue
Polyester stuffing
1 small bell
Embroidery cotton
1 pair of 8 mm (⅜ in) diameter wobbly eyes

1. Transfer the pattern on page 95 on to tracing paper and cut out. Pin the pattern to the fabric and cut two body pieces, and two hand pieces and two foot pieces from white fabric.

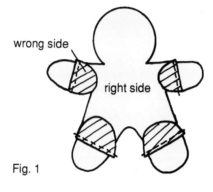

Fig. 1

2. Sew the hand and foot pieces to the one body section as shown in fig. 1. Fold the white pieces over to the front and tack in place around the edges as shown in fig. 2.

Fig. 2

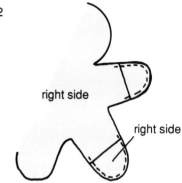

3. Cut a 14 cm (5½ in) length of ribbon for the hanging loop. Bring the ribbon ends together and tack them to the one body piece as shown in fig. 3.

Fig. 3

4. Sew the ric-rac braid over the seams joining the white hand and foot pieces to the body piece.

5. With right sides together, join the two body pieces, leaving a gap in the seam as indicated on the pattern. Clip into the curves and turn through. Remove the tacking thread.

6. Stuff the body firmly and sew the gap in the seam closed.

7. Glue a length of ric-rac braid around the edge of the face to the neck level at each side.

8. Thread the bell on to a length of ribbon and tie it around the neck, making a bow at the front.

9. Cut out a nose, two heart-shaped cheeks and two 'buttons' from felt. Glue on the nose, embroider the mouth, then glue on the cheeks, wobbly eyes and felt 'buttons'.

Elf Christmas tree ornament

These cute elves are lovely to hang on the Christmas tree and are good stocking-fillers too.

Fig. 2

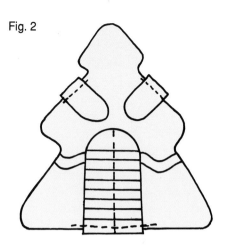

REQUIREMENTS
(FOR EACH ELF)

Green fabric off-cuts for the elf tree body

Red and white stripe fabric off-cut for the legs

Fabric scraps for the shoes

Scraps of flesh-coloured and brown felt for the face piece

25 cm (9⅞ in) of 8 mm (⅜ in) wide ribbon for the hanging loop and the bow-tie

Red embroidery cotton

1 pair of tiny wobbly eyes

Polyester stuffing

Glue

Trimming for decorating the elf tree body, such as gold or silver ric-rac and sequins

1 bell

3. *To make the tree body*, transfer the patterns on page 94 on to tracing paper and cut out. Pin the traced patterns to the fabric and cut one tree front and two tree backs from green fabric; cut two hands and one face from flesh-coloured felt.

4. With right sides together join the two back pieces together, leaving a gap in the seam, as indicated on the pattern. Sew the ric-rac braid to the tree front piece. Tack the hands and the legs in position as shown in fig. 2.

5. With right sides together, sew the tree front and back together round the outer edge incorporating the hands and legs into the seams. Clip into the curves and turn through, through the gap in the back seam. Stuff firmly and sew the gap in the seam closed.

6. Sew a 16 cm (6¼ in) loop of ribbon to the top of the head for hanging.

7. Sew the felt face piece to the tree body. Using two strands of red embroidery cotton, embroider a little mouth and a nose. Glue on the wobbly eyes. Glue on a scrap of brown felt for a fringe.

8. Glue sequins and stars to the tree. Glue a ribbon bow at the chin. Sew the bell to the feet.

1. *To make the legs*, cut two pieces from the striped fabric, each measuring 5 cm x 5 cm (2 in x 2 in). For the shoes, transfer the pattern on page 94 on to tracing paper and cut out. Pin the traced pattern to the fabric and cut out two shoe pieces.

2. With right sides together, sew a shoe piece to each leg piece, with the stripes running in a horizontal direction. With right sides together, join the two leg pieces round the outer edge, leaving the top edge open. Turn through and stuff lightly. Topstitch down the centre of the fabric to form legs, as shown in fig. 1.

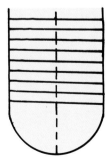

Fig. 1

Christmas card holder

A decorative way to display your Christmas cards. It would look wonderful hanging from your mantelpiece. Cut the ribbon to the lengths of your choice.

REQUIREMENTS
60 cm x 29 cm (23⅝ in x 11½ in) of red fabric for the arms
Polyester stuffing
50 cm (19¾ in) of 12 mm (½ in) diameter dowel rod
2.5 m (98 in) of 24 mm (1 in) wide ribbon or more if you want longer ribbons
5 large bells
26 cm x 34 cm (10¾ in x 13½ in) of fabric for the hands
44 cm x 22 cm (17⅜ in x 8⅝ in) of flesh-coloured fabric for the head
50 cm x 30 cm (19¾ in x 12 in) of white fake fur fabric for the beard and trim
Scraps of red, green and pink felt
1 pair of 12 mm (½ in) diameter wobbly eyes
Glue
6 cm (2⅓ in) diameter circle of red fabric for the nose
36 cm x 44 cm (14¼ in x 17⅜ in) of red fabric for the hat
Loop of tape for hanging the holder

1. *To make the arms*, cut one piece of red fabric 60 cm x 12 cm (23⅝ in x 4¾ in), and a second piece 60 cm x 17 cm (23⅝ in x 6¾ in).

2. Turn in a 1 cm (⅜ in) hem at the short edges of each piece and sew in place.

3. With wrong sides together, fold the wider piece in half lengthwise and sew a seam 2.5 cm (1 in) from the fold, to form the dowel tube, as shown in fig. 1.

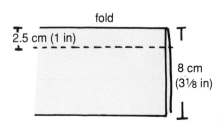

Fig. 1

4. Cut five 50 cm (19¾ in) lengths of 24 mm (1 in) wide ribbon – or longer if you wish. Tack the ends of the ribbons to the long edge of the narrower arm piece, as shown in fig. 2.

Fig. 2

5. With right sides together, join the arm tubes along the long edges, being careful not to catch the ribbon ends into the top of the seam.

6. Turn through and stuff the arms firmly.

7. *To make the hands*, transfer the pattern on page 94 on to tracing paper and cut out. Pin the traced pattern to the fabric and cut four hand pieces.

8. With right sides together, join the hand pieces in pairs, leaving the wrist edges open. Turn through and stuff the hands.

9. Run a gathering thread round the wrist edges, pull up the gathers tightly and sew off securely.

10. Insert the hands into each end of the arm tube. Pin them in position and sew the arm ends neatly to the hands, leaving the length of dowel tube on the back arm piece free.

11. *To make the head*, cut two 22 cm (8⅝ in) diameter circles from the flesh-coloured fabric. With right sides together, join the two pieces round the outer edge, leaving a gap in the seam.

12. Turn through and stuff the head. Sew the gap in the seam closed.

13. *To make the hat*, cut two pieces of fabric as shown in fig. 3.

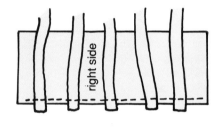

Fig. 3

14. With right sides together, join the hat pieces along the side seams, leaving the head edge open. Turn through.

15. Pin the hat to the head, pulling it well down at the back of the head. Sew the hat in place.

16. Cut a 50 cm (19¾ in) long strip of fake fur fabric, 3.5 cm (1½ in) wide. Glue this strip round the hat, where it is sewn to the head, with the join positioned at the back of the head.

17. *To make the beard and moustache*, transfer the patterns on page 94 on to tracing paper and cut out. Pin the traced patterns to the white fake fur fabric and cut out one beard and one moustache.

18. Glue the beard along its top edge to the face, with the top of the sides of the beard immediately under the hat trim.

19. Cut a mouth from red felt and glue it in place. Glue the moustache centre to the face.

20. *To make the nose*, run a gathering thread round the outer edge of the 6 cm (2⅓ in) diameter circle of red fabric. Put a ball of stuffing into the centre, pull up the gathers tightly and sew off securely. Glue the nose to the face at the centre of the moustache.

21. Cut two cheeks (*see* pattern on page 94) from pink felt and glue them to the face in their correct position.

22. Glue on the wobbly eyes in their correct position.

23. *To make the eyebrows*, cut two small strips of white fake fur fabric and glue them above the eyes.

24. Cut two 3.5 cm (1½ in) wide strips of white fake fur, each measuring 25 cm (9⅞ in) in length. Glue these strips round the wrists.

25. Sew a bell to the end of each length of ribbon.

26. Insert the dowel rod into the tube at the back of the arms.

27. Attach the head to the arms.

28. Cut two holly leaves (*see* pattern on page 94) from green felt and three red circles from red felt, for the berries. Glue them to the fur strip around the hat.

29. *To make the hat's pompon*, cut a 10 cm (4 in) diameter circle from white fake fur fabric. Run a gathering thread round the outer edge and put a ball of stuffing into the centre. Pull up the gathers tightly and sew off securely.

30. Fold the hat down to the one side of the head and glue it in place. Glue the pompon to the point of the hat.

31. Sew a loop of tape to the centre back of the arms to hang the card holder.

Goose Christmas tree ornament

Make a gaggle of these for your tree. You can make them in any colour and decorate them with sequins and beads.

REQUIREMENTS
(FOR EACH GOOSE)

White fabric off-cuts for the body
Scrap of yellow fabric for the beak
Polyester filling
50 cm (19¾ in) of 8 mm (⅜ in) wide
  ribbon for the legs, the hanging
  loop and the neck bow
1 small bell
Felt off-cuts for the wings
Glue
2 black sequins

1. Transfer the patterns on page 95 on to tracing paper and cut out. Pin the traced patterns to the fabric and cut out two body pieces from white fabric, two beak pieces from yellow fabric and two wings from felt.

2. Cut a 10 cm (4 in) length of ribbon for the legs. Thread the bell on to the ribbon. Bring the ribbon ends together and tack them to one of the body pieces at the position indicated on the pattern, as shown in fig. 1.

3. Cut a 16 cm (6¼ in) length of ribbon for the hanging loop. Bring the ends of the ribbon together and tack them to the body piece in the position indicated on the pattern, as shown in fig. 1.

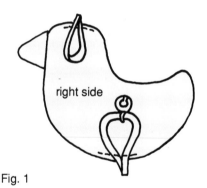

Fig. 1

4. With right sides together, join the two body pieces, leaving a gap in the seam as indicated on the pattern. Clip into the curves and turn through. Stuff the body and sew the gap in the seam closed.

5. Tie a ribbon round the neck, making a bow at the front.

6. Glue on the sequin eyes. Glue on the wings, leaving the wing tips free.

Patterns

The following pages contain all the patterns needed to make the toys.

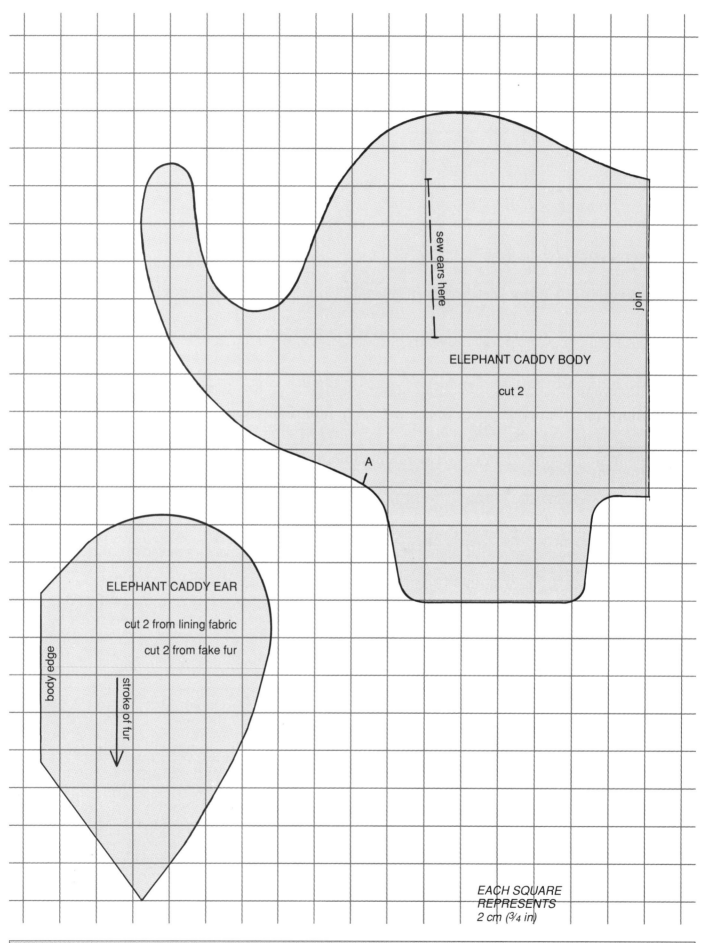

sew ears here

join

ELEPHANT CADDY BODY

cut 2

A

ELEPHANT CADDY EAR

cut 2 from lining fabric

cut 2 from fake fur

body edge

stroke of fur

EACH SQUARE
REPRESENTS
2 cm (¾ in)

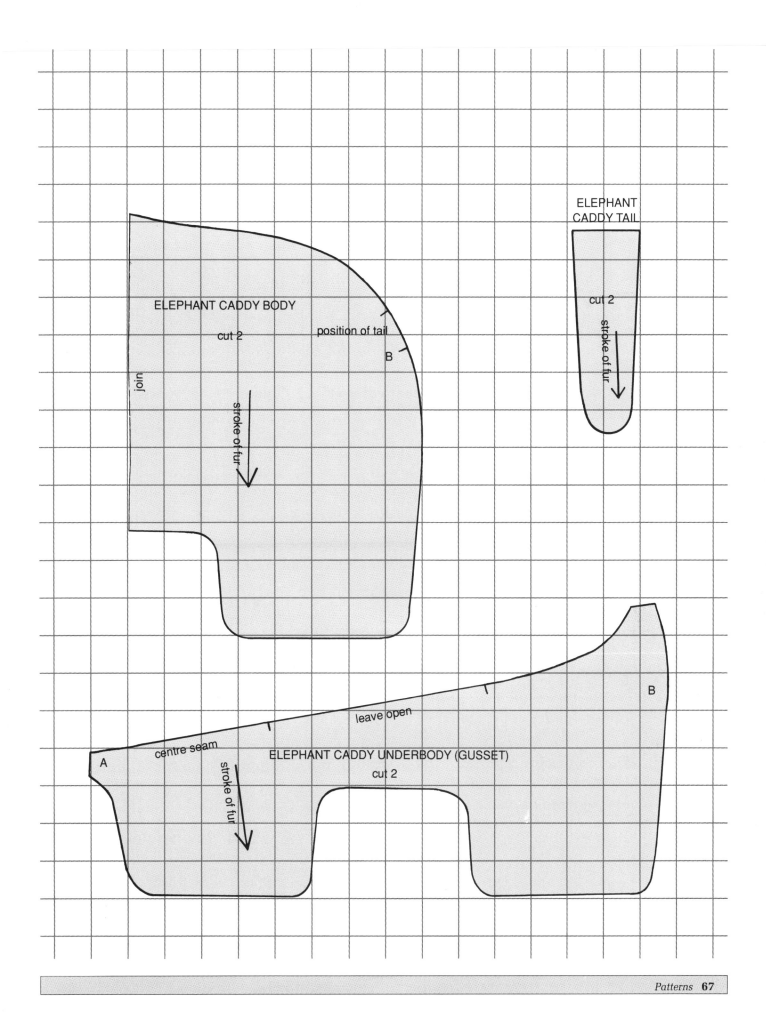

ELEPHANT
CADDY TAIL

cut 2

stroke of fur

ELEPHANT CADDY BODY

cut 2

position of tail

B

join

stroke of fur

B

leave open

A

centre seam

ELEPHANT CADDY UNDERBODY (GUSSET)

cut 2

stroke of fur

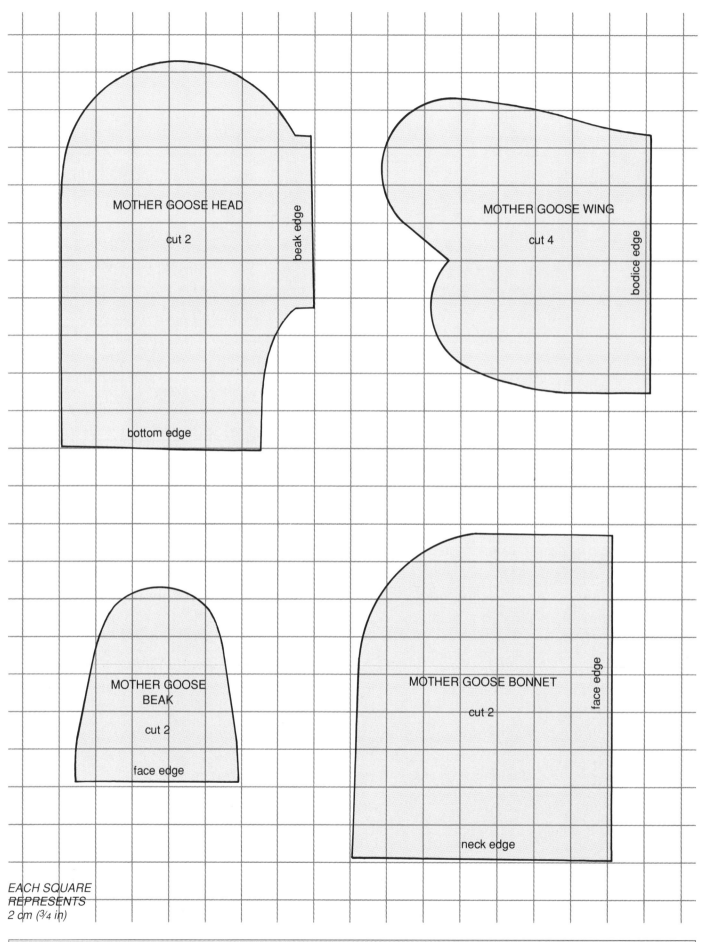

MOTHER GOOSE HEAD

cut 2

beak edge

bottom edge

MOTHER GOOSE WING

cut 4

bodice edge

MOTHER GOOSE
BEAK

cut 2

face edge

MOTHER GOOSE BONNET

cut 2

face edge

neck edge

EACH SQUARE
REPRESENTS
2 cm (¾ in)

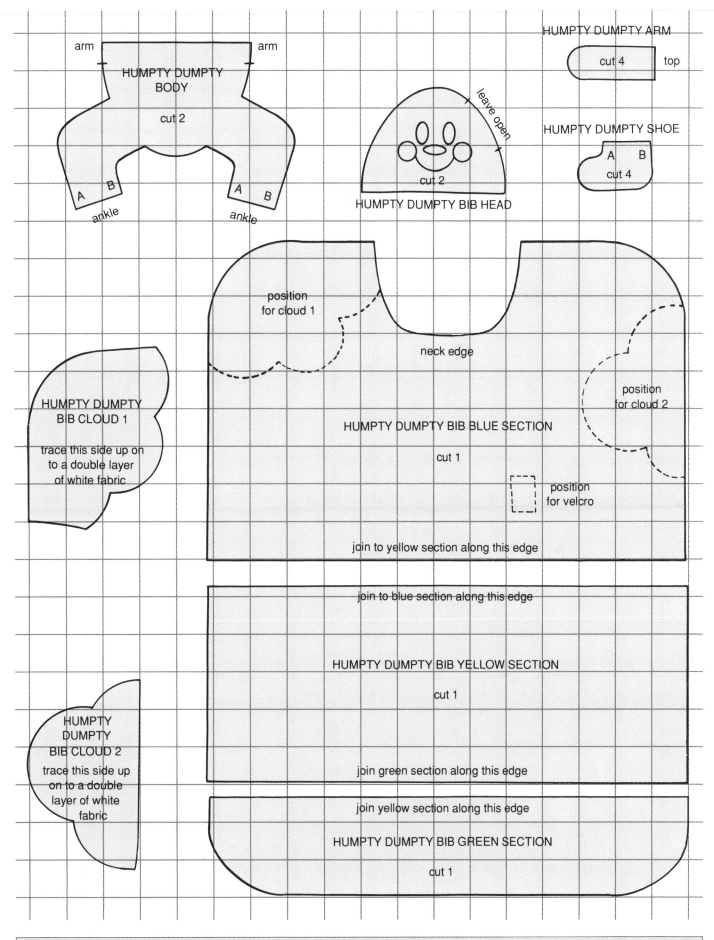

HUMPTY DUMPTY ARM

cut 4   top

arm   arm

HUMPTY DUMPTY
BODY

cut 2

leave open

A   B   A   B

ankle   ankle

HUMPTY DUMPTY SHOE

A   B

cut 4

cut 2

HUMPTY DUMPTY BIB HEAD

position
for cloud 1

neck edge

position
for cloud 2

HUMPTY DUMPTY
BIB CLOUD 1

trace this side up on
to a double layer
of white fabric

HUMPTY DUMPTY BIB BLUE SECTION

cut 1

position
for velcro

join to yellow section along this edge

join to blue section along this edge

HUMPTY DUMPTY BIB YELLOW SECTION

cut 1

HUMPTY
DUMPTY
BIB CLOUD 2

trace this side up
on to a double
layer of white
fabric

join green section along this edge

join yellow section along this edge

HUMPTY DUMPTY BIB GREEN SECTION

cut 1

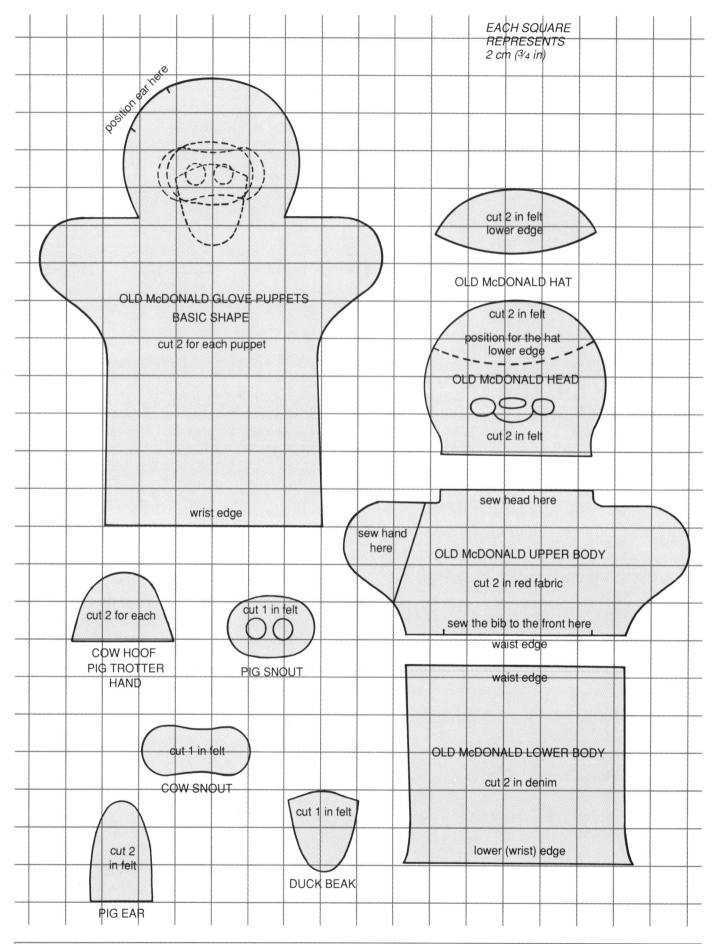

EACH SQUARE
REPRESENTS
2 cm (¾ in)

position ear here

OLD McDONALD GLOVE PUPPETS
BASIC SHAPE

cut 2 for each puppet

wrist edge

cut 2 in felt
lower edge

OLD McDONALD HAT

cut 2 in felt

position for the hat
lower edge

OLD McDONALD HEAD

cut 2 in felt

sew head here

sew hand
here

OLD McDONALD UPPER BODY

cut 2 in red fabric

sew the bib to the front here

waist edge

cut 2 for each

COW HOOF
PIG TROTTER
HAND

cut 1 in felt

PIG SNOUT

cut 1 in felt

COW SNOUT

cut 2
in felt

PIG EAR

cut 1 in felt

DUCK BEAK

waist edge

OLD McDONALD LOWER BODY

cut 2 in denim

lower (wrist) edge

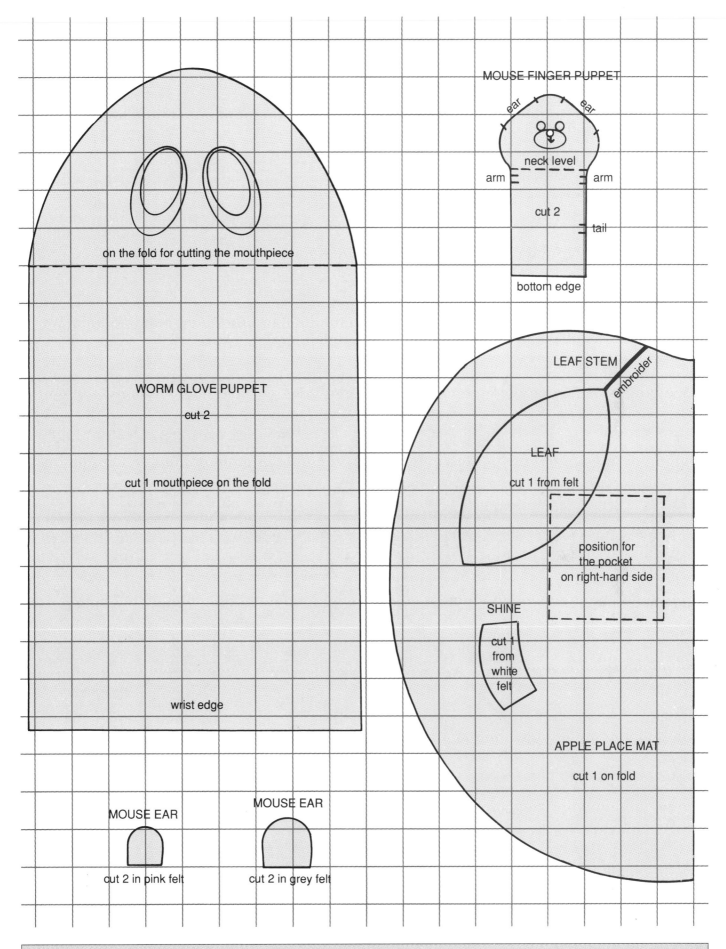

MOUSE FINGER PUPPET

ear   ear

neck level

arm   arm

cut 2

tail

bottom edge

on the fold for cutting the mouthpiece

LEAF STEM

embroider

LEAF

cut 1 from felt

position for
the pocket
on right-hand side

WORM GLOVE PUPPET

cut 2

cut 1 mouthpiece on the fold

SHINE

cut 1
from
white
felt

wrist edge

APPLE PLACE MAT

cut 1 on fold

MOUSE EAR

MOUSE EAR

cut 2 in pink felt

cut 2 in grey felt

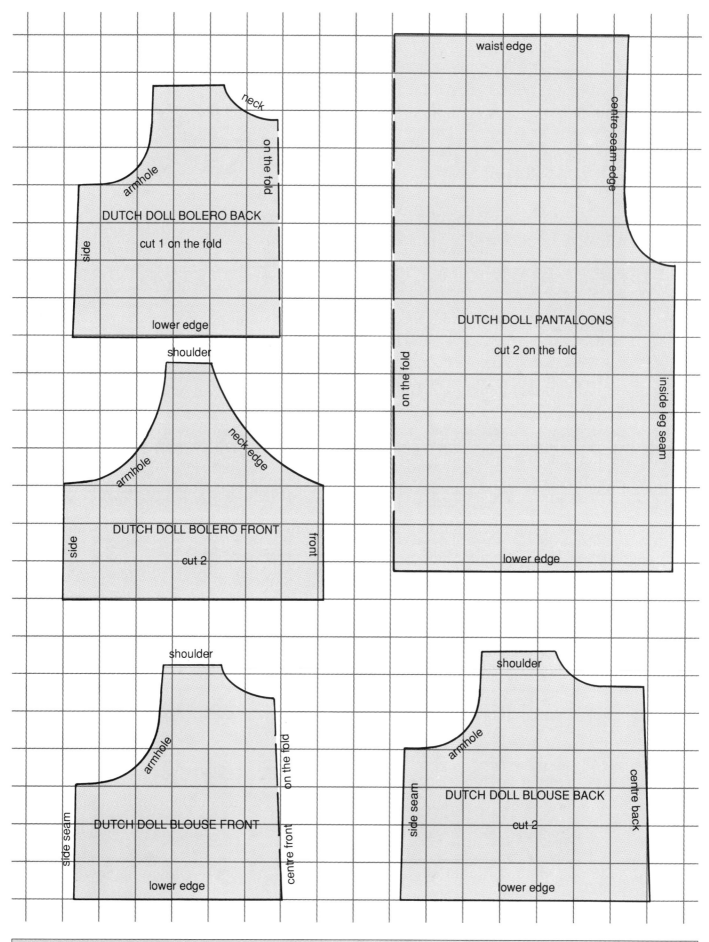

DUTCH DOLL BOLERO BACK

neck

on the fold

armhole

side

cut 1 on the fold

lower edge

shoulder

neck edge

armhole

side

DUTCH DOLL BOLERO FRONT

front

cut 2

waist edge

centre seam edge

on the fold

DUTCH DOLL PANTALOONS

cut 2 on the fold

inside leg seam

lower edge

shoulder

armhole

side seam

DUTCH DOLL BLOUSE FRONT

on the fold

centre front

lower edge

shoulder

armhole

side seam

DUTCH DOLL BLOUSE BACK

centre back

cut 2

lower edge

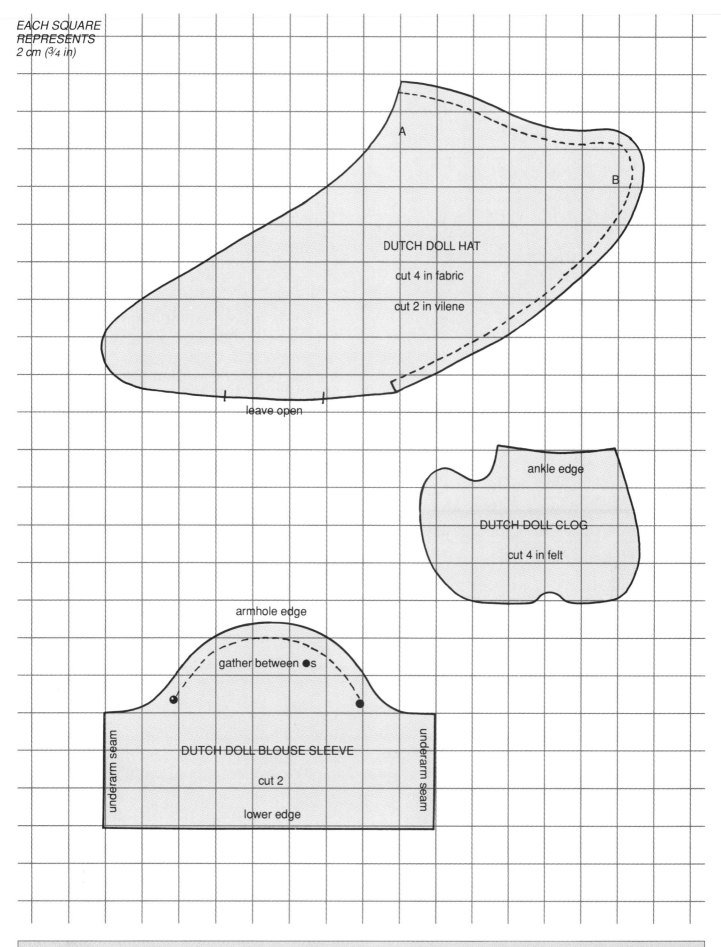

EACH SQUARE
REPRESENTS
2 cm (¾ in)

A

B

DUTCH DOLL HAT

cut 4 in fabric

cut 2 in vilene

leave open

ankle edge

DUTCH DOLL CLOG

cut 4 in felt

armhole edge

gather between ●s

underarm seam

DUTCH DOLL BLOUSE SLEEVE

cut 2

underarm seam

lower edge

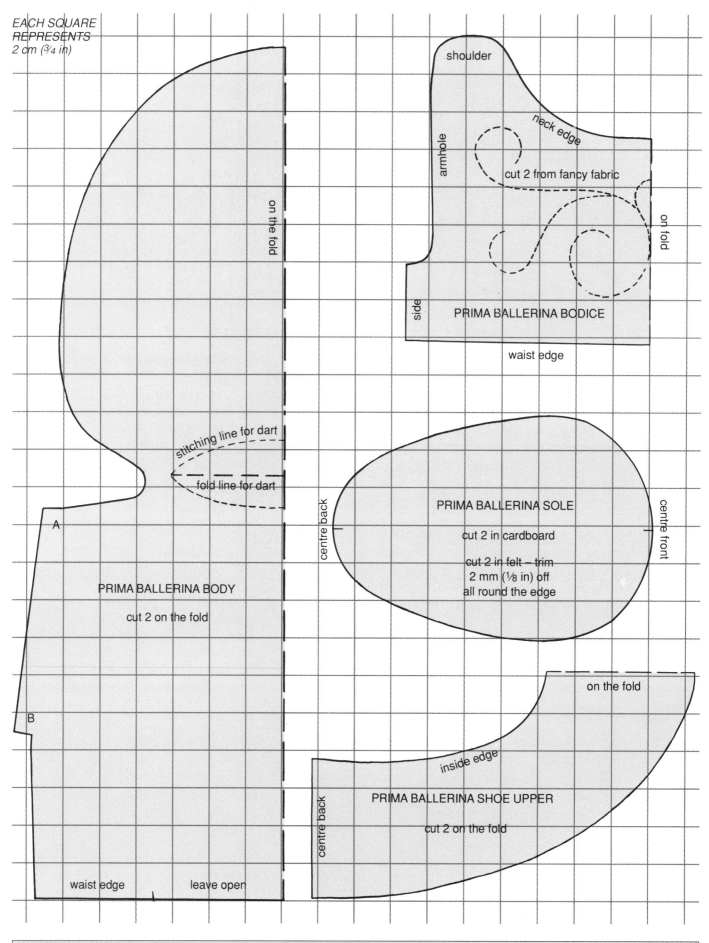

EACH SQUARE
REPRESENTS
2 cm (¾ in)

shoulder

neck edge

armhole

on fold

cut 2 from fancy fabric

side

PRIMA BALLERINA BODICE

waist edge

on the fold

stitching line for dart

fold line for dart

A

PRIMA BALLERINA BODY

cut 2 on the fold

centre back

PRIMA BALLERINA SOLE

cut 2 in cardboard

cut 2 in felt – trim
2 mm (⅛ in) off
all round the edge

centre front

on the fold

B

inside edge

centre back

PRIMA BALLERINA SHOE UPPER

cut 2 on the fold

waist edge   leave open

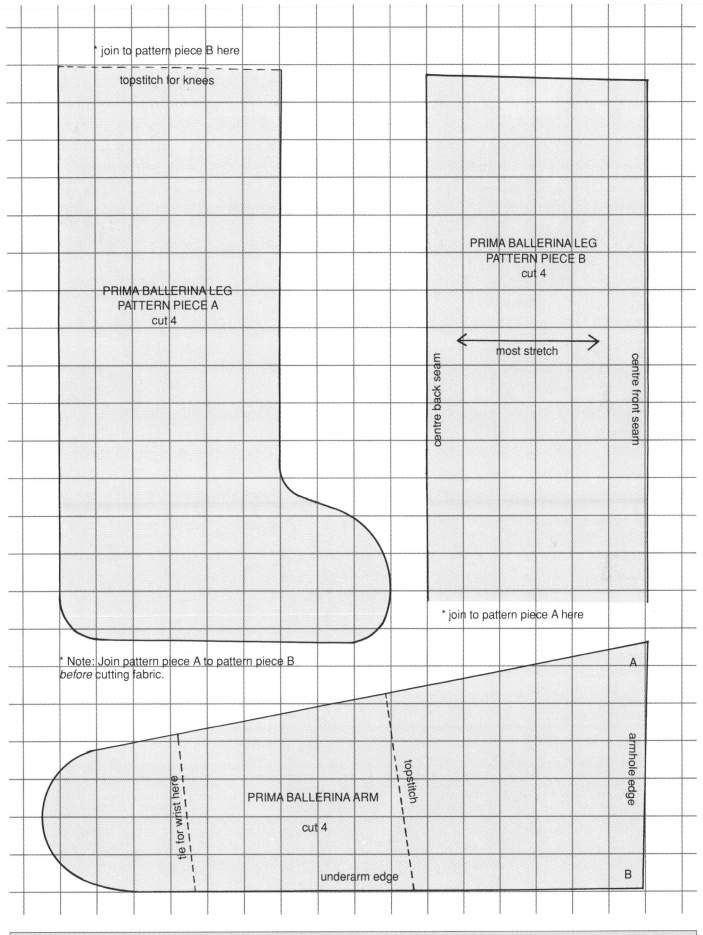

* join to pattern piece B here

topstitch for knees

PRIMA BALLERINA LEG
PATTERN PIECE A
cut 4

PRIMA BALLERINA LEG
PATTERN PIECE B
cut 4

most stretch

centre back seam

centre front seam

* join to pattern piece A here

* Note: Join pattern piece A to pattern piece B
before cutting fabric.

A

armhole edge

PRIMA BALLERINA ARM

cut 4

tie for wrist here

topstitch

underarm edge

B

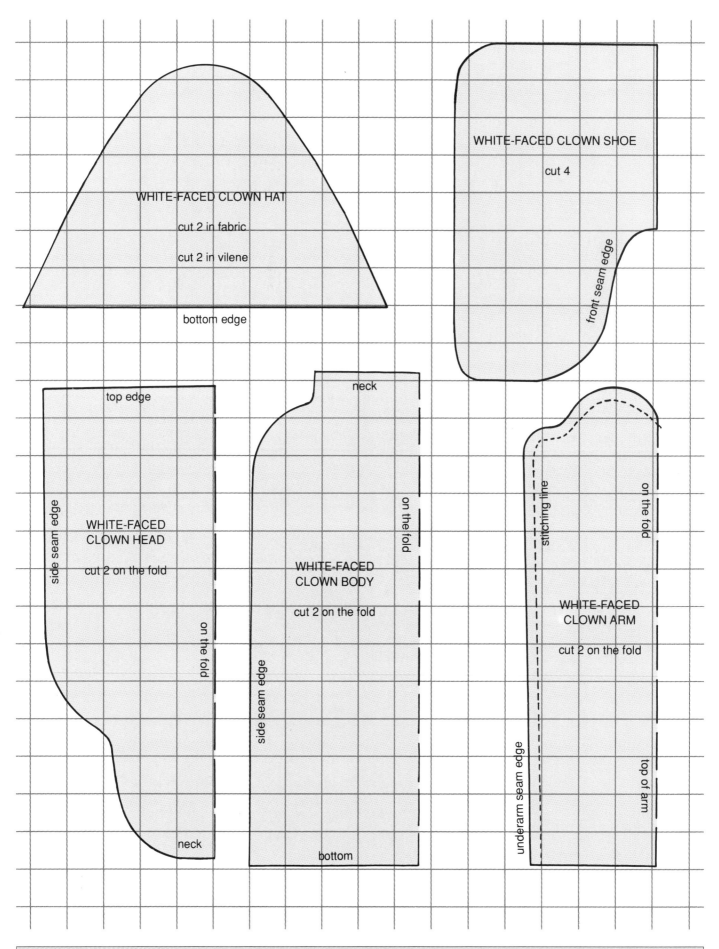

WHITE-FACED CLOWN HAT

cut 2 in fabric

cut 2 in vilene

bottom edge

WHITE-FACED CLOWN SHOE

cut 4

front seam edge

top edge

side seam edge

WHITE-FACED
CLOWN HEAD

cut 2 on the fold

on the fold

neck

neck

on the fold

WHITE-FACED
CLOWN BODY

cut 2 on the fold

side seam edge

bottom

stitching line

on the fold

WHITE-FACED
CLOWN ARM

cut 2 on the fold

underarm seam edge

top of arm

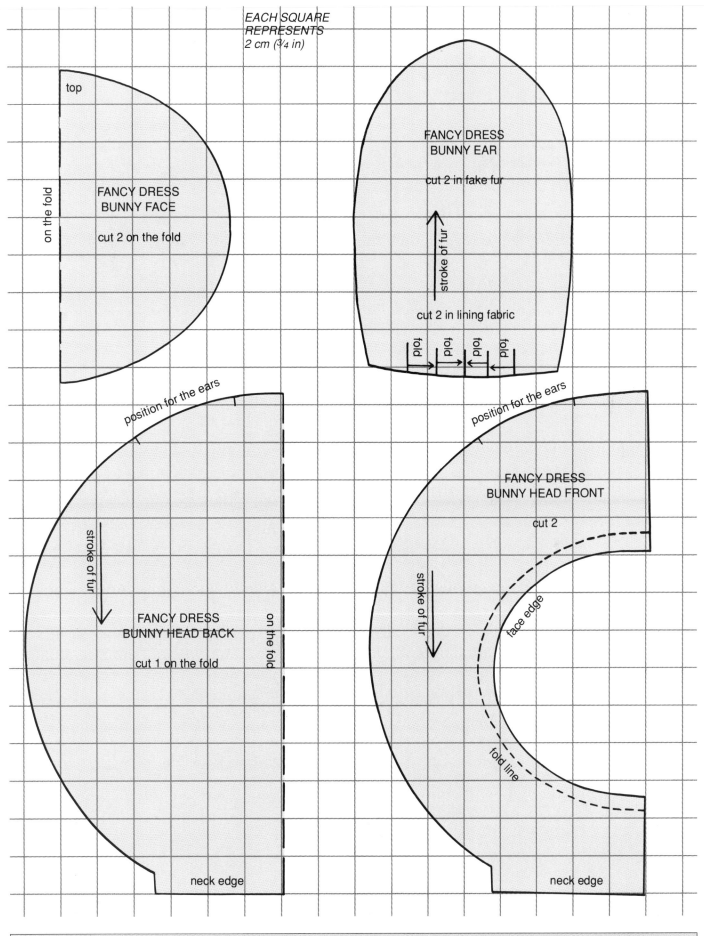

EACH SQUARE
REPRESENTS
2 cm (¾ in)

top

on the fold

FANCY DRESS
BUNNY FACE

cut 2 on the fold

FANCY DRESS
BUNNY EAR

cut 2 in fake fur

stroke of fur

cut 2 in lining fabric

fold   fold   fold   fold

position for the ears

position for the ears

stroke of fur

FANCY DRESS
BUNNY HEAD BACK

cut 1 on the fold

on the fold

neck edge

FANCY DRESS
BUNNY HEAD FRONT

cut 2

stroke of fur

face edge

fold line

neck edge

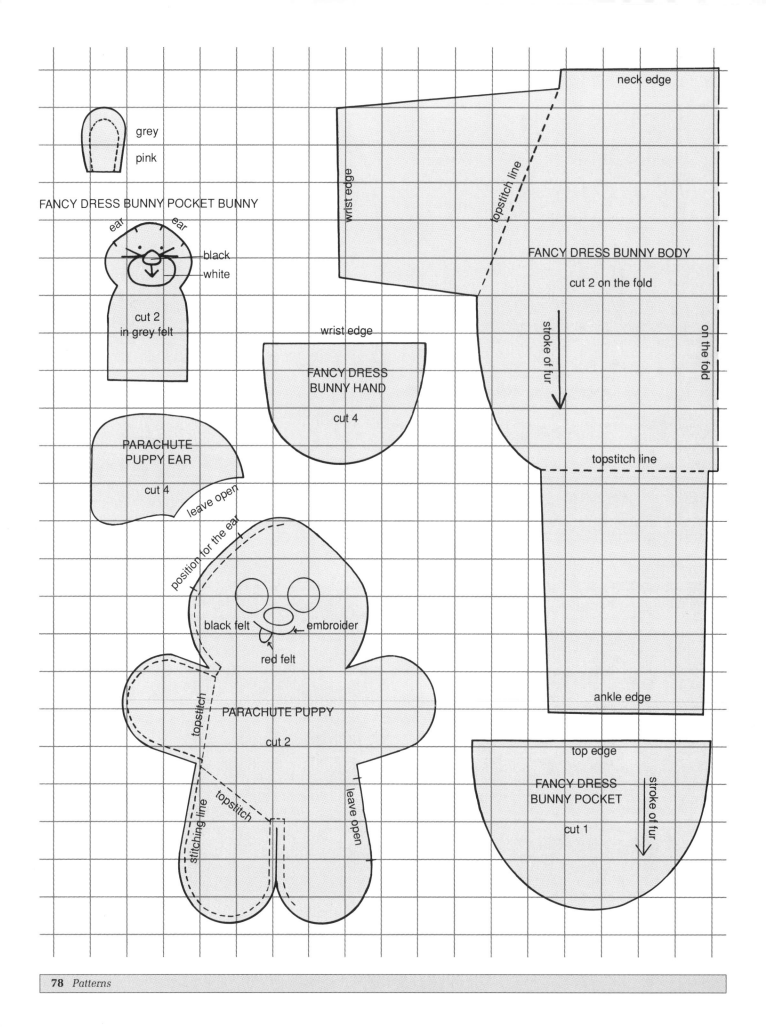

grey

pink

FANCY DRESS BUNNY POCKET BUNNY

ear   ear

black

white

cut 2
in grey felt

neck edge

wrist edge

topstitch line

FANCY DRESS BUNNY BODY

cut 2 on the fold

stroke of fur

on the fold

wrist edge

FANCY DRESS
BUNNY HAND

cut 4

PARACHUTE
PUPPY EAR

cut 4

leave open

topstitch line

position for the ear

black felt

embroider

red felt

topstitch

PARACHUTE PUPPY

cut 2

ankle edge

top edge

FANCY DRESS
BUNNY POCKET

cut 1

stroke of fur

stitching line

topstitch

leave open

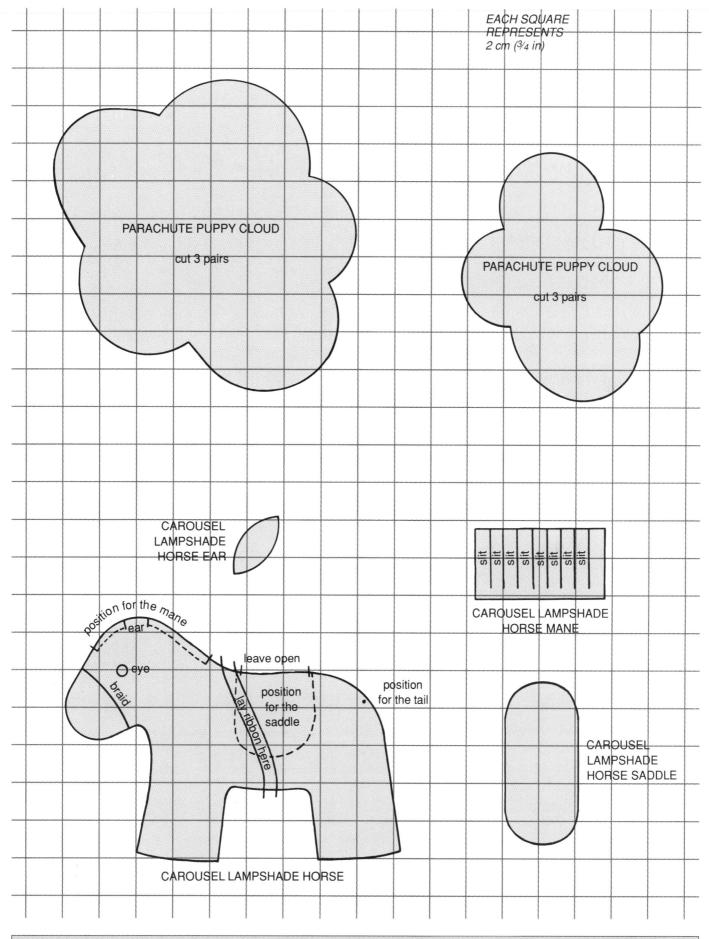

EACH SQUARE
REPRESENTS
2 cm (³⁄₄ in)

PARACHUTE PUPPY CLOUD

cut 3 pairs

PARACHUTE PUPPY CLOUD

cut 3 pairs

CAROUSEL
LAMPSHADE
HORSE EAR

CAROUSEL LAMPSHADE
HORSE MANE

slit slit slit slit slit slit slit slit

position for the mane

ear

leave open

eye

braid

lay ribbon here

position
for the
saddle

position
for the tail

CAROUSEL
LAMPSHADE
HORSE SADDLE

CAROUSEL LAMPSHADE HORSE

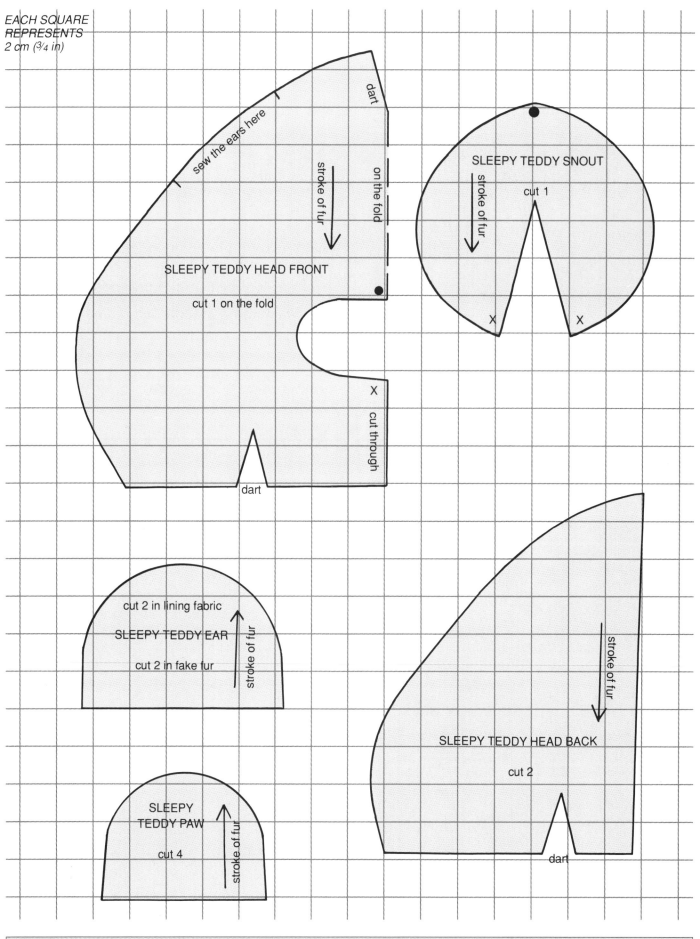

EACH SQUARE
REPRESENTS
2 cm (¾ in)

sew the ears here

dart

stroke of fur

on the fold

SLEEPY TEDDY SNOUT

stroke of fur

cut 1

SLEEPY TEDDY HEAD FRONT

cut 1 on the fold

X

cut through

X   X

dart

cut 2 in lining fabric

SLEEPY TEDDY EAR

cut 2 in fake fur

stroke of fur

stroke of fur

SLEEPY
TEDDY HEAD BACK

cut 2

SLEEPY
TEDDY PAW

cut 4

stroke of fur

dart

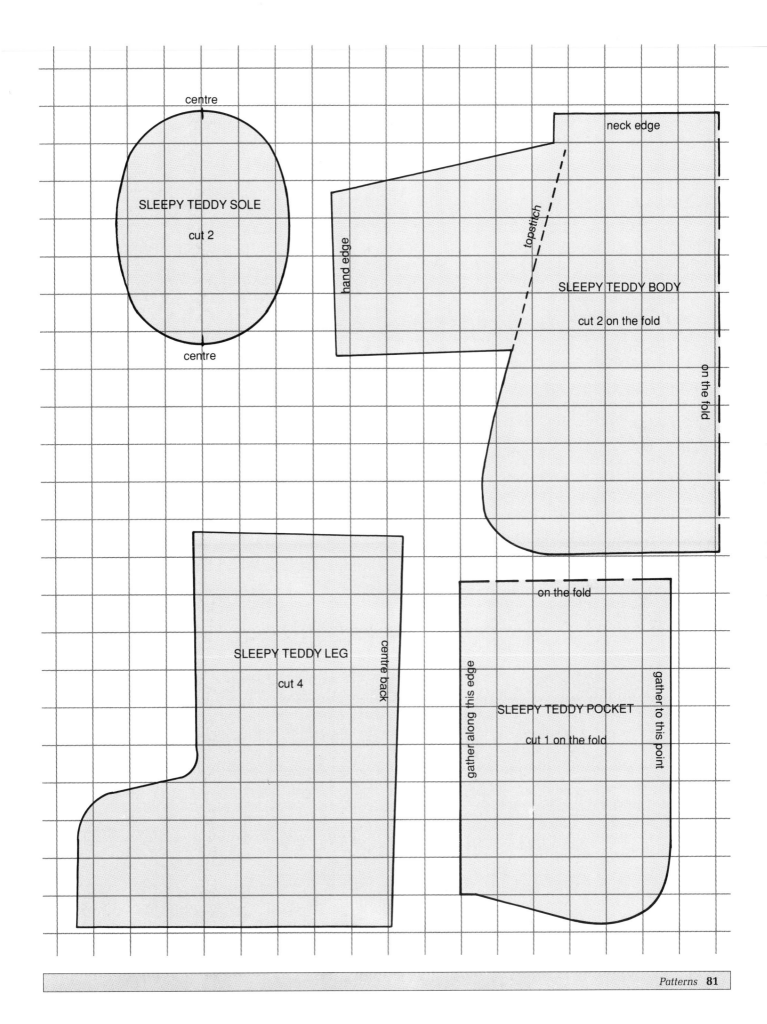

SLEEPY TEDDY SOLE

cut 2

centre

centre

SLEEPY TEDDY BODY

cut 2 on the fold

neck edge

hand edge

topstitch

on the fold

SLEEPY TEDDY LEG

cut 4

centre back

SLEEPY TEDDY POCKET

cut 1 on the fold

on the fold

gather along this edge

gather to this point

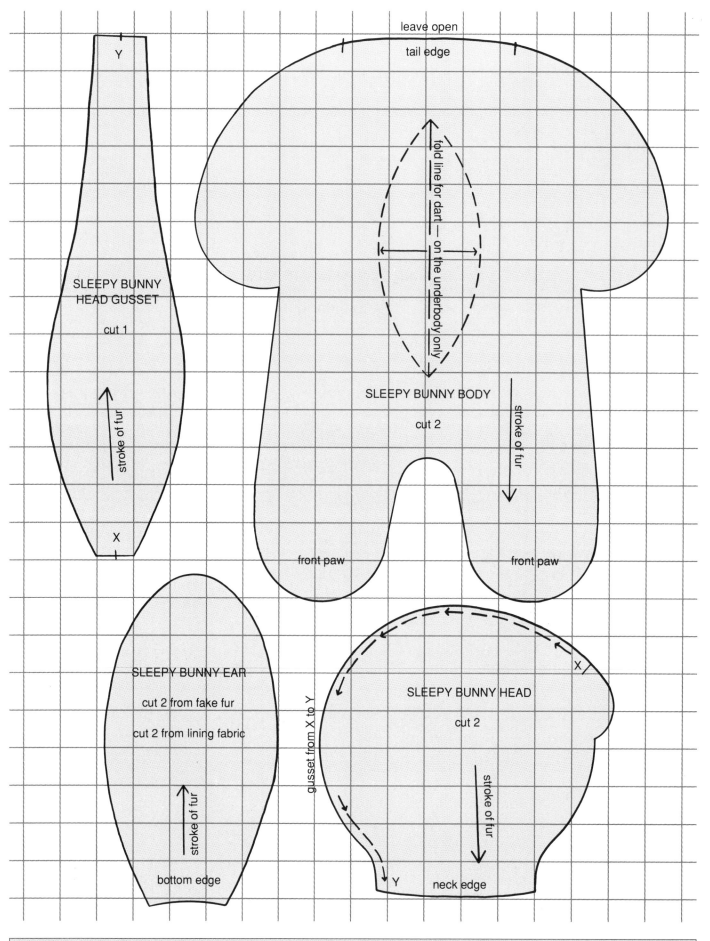

SLEEPY BUNNY
HEAD GUSSET

cut 1

stroke of fur

Y

X

leave open

tail edge

fold line for dart — on the underbody only

SLEEPY BUNNY BODY

cut 2

stroke of fur

front paw

front paw

SLEEPY BUNNY EAR

cut 2 from fake fur

cut 2 from lining fabric

stroke of fur

bottom edge

gusset from X to Y

SLEEPY BUNNY HEAD

cut 2

X

stroke of fur

Y

neck edge

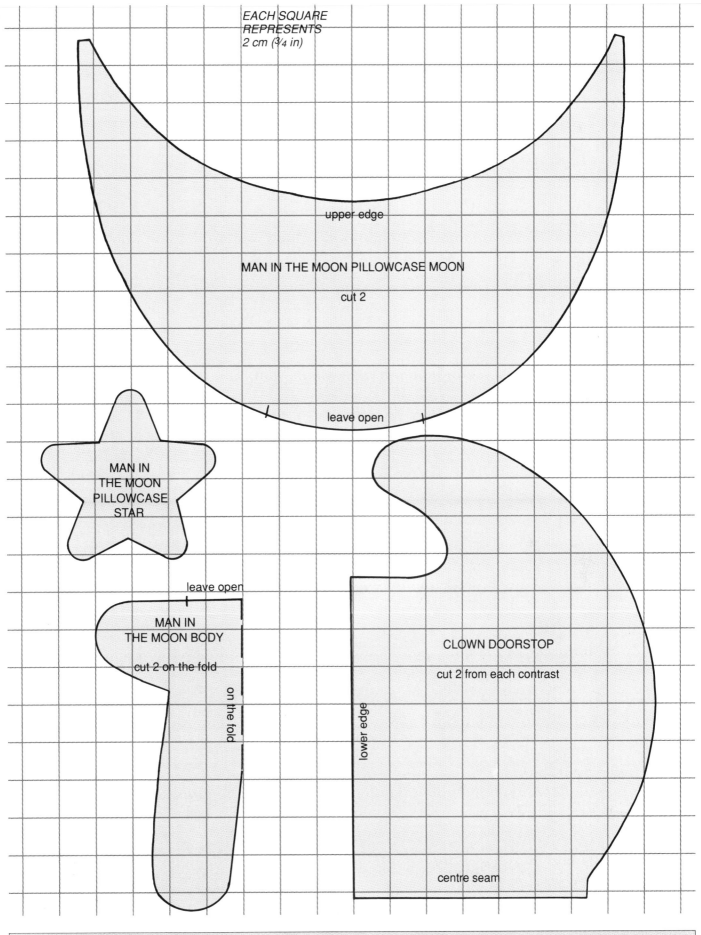

EACH SQUARE
REPRESENTS
2 cm (¾ in)

upper edge

MAN IN THE MOON PILLOWCASE MOON

cut 2

leave open

MAN IN
THE MOON
PILLOWCASE
STAR

leave open

MAN IN
THE MOON BODY

cut 2 on the fold

on the fold

CLOWN DOORSTOP

cut 2 from each contrast

lower edge

centre seam

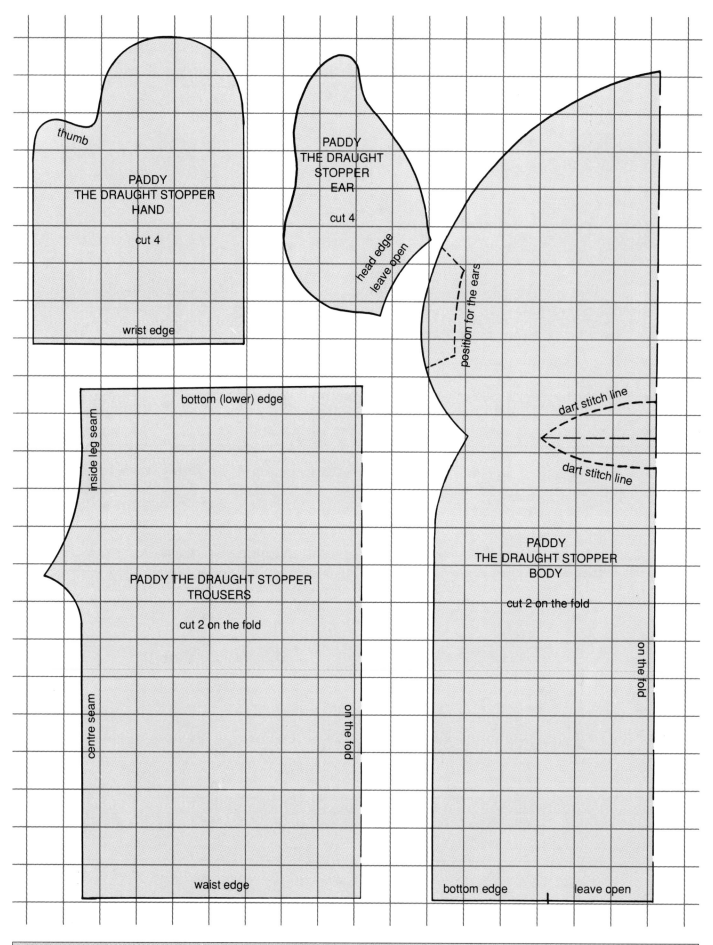

thumb

PADDY
THE DRAUGHT STOPPER
HAND

cut 4

wrist edge

PADDY
THE DRAUGHT
STOPPER
EAR

cut 4

head edge
leave open

position for the ears

dart stitch line

dart stitch line

bottom (lower) edge

inside leg seam

PADDY THE DRAUGHT STOPPER
TROUSERS

cut 2 on the fold

centre seam

on the fold

waist edge

PADDY
THE DRAUGHT STOPPER
BODY

cut 2 on the fold

on the fold

bottom edge

leave open

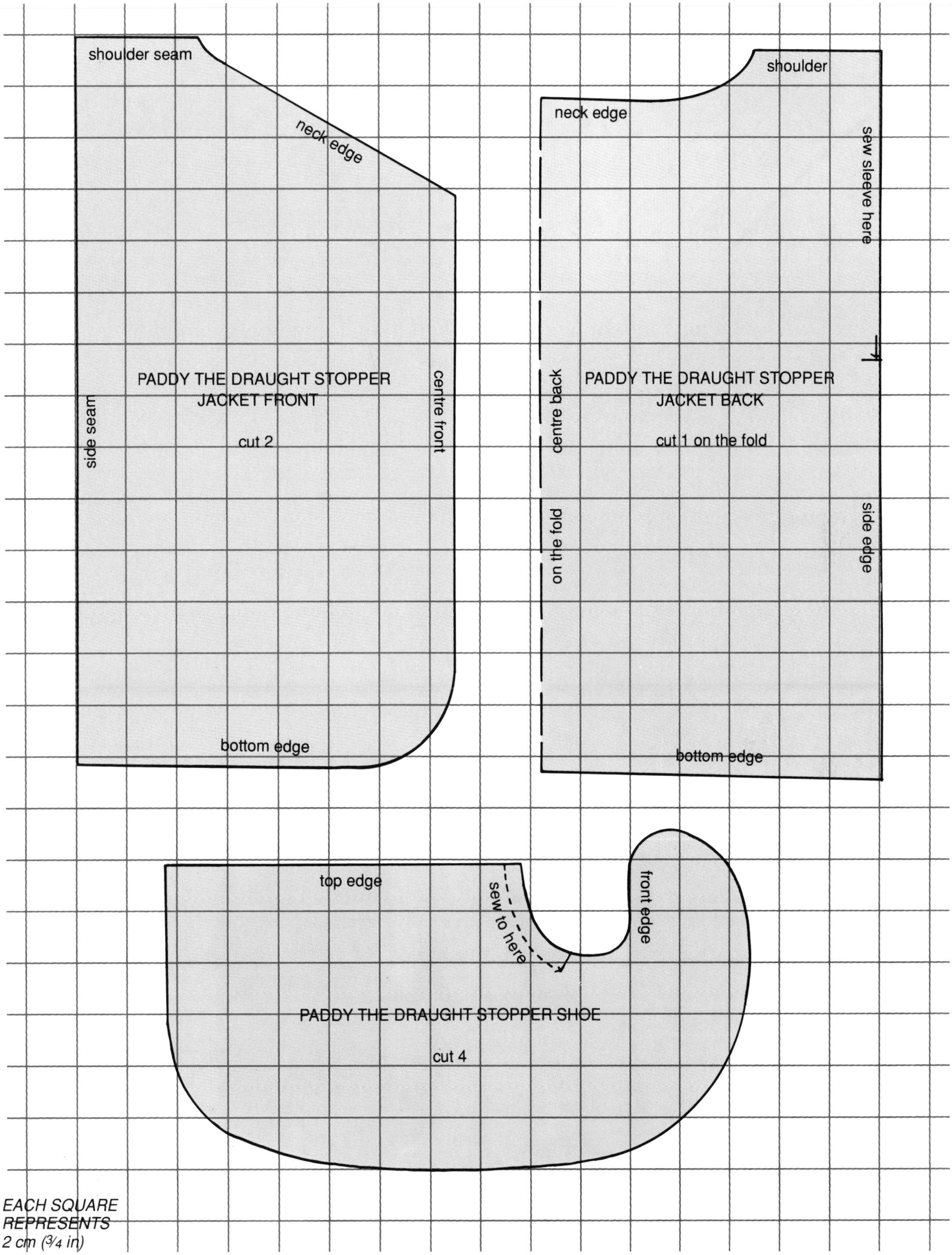

shoulder seam

neck edge

shoulder

neck edge

sew sleeve here

side seam

PADDY THE DRAUGHT STOPPER

JACKET FRONT

cut 2

centre front

centre back

on the fold

PADDY THE DRAUGHT STOPPER

JACKET BACK

cut 1 on the fold

side edge

bottom edge

bottom edge

top edge

sew to here

front edge

PADDY THE DRAUGHT STOPPER SHOE

cut 4

EACH SQUARE
REPRESENTS
2 cm (¾ in)

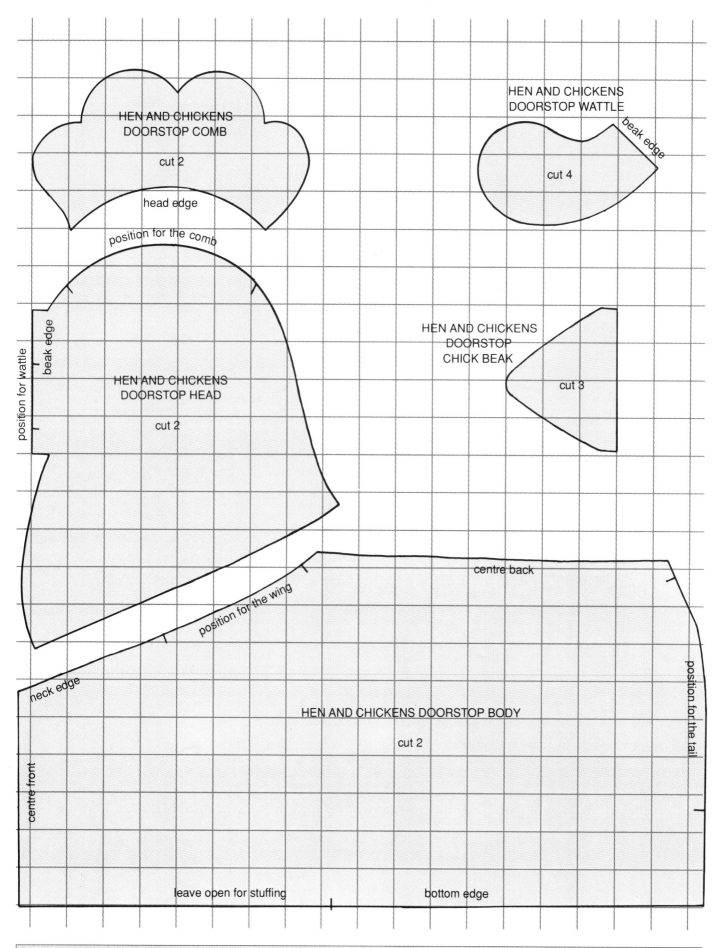

HEN AND CHICKENS
DOORSTOP COMB

cut 2

head edge

HEN AND CHICKENS
DOORSTOP WATTLE

beak edge

cut 4

position for the comb

position for wattle

beak edge

HEN AND CHICKENS
DOORSTOP HEAD

cut 2

HEN AND CHICKENS
DOORSTOP
CHICK BEAK

cut 3

centre back

position for the wing

position for the tail

neck edge

HEN AND CHICKENS DOORSTOP BODY

cut 2

centre front

leave open for stuffing

bottom edge

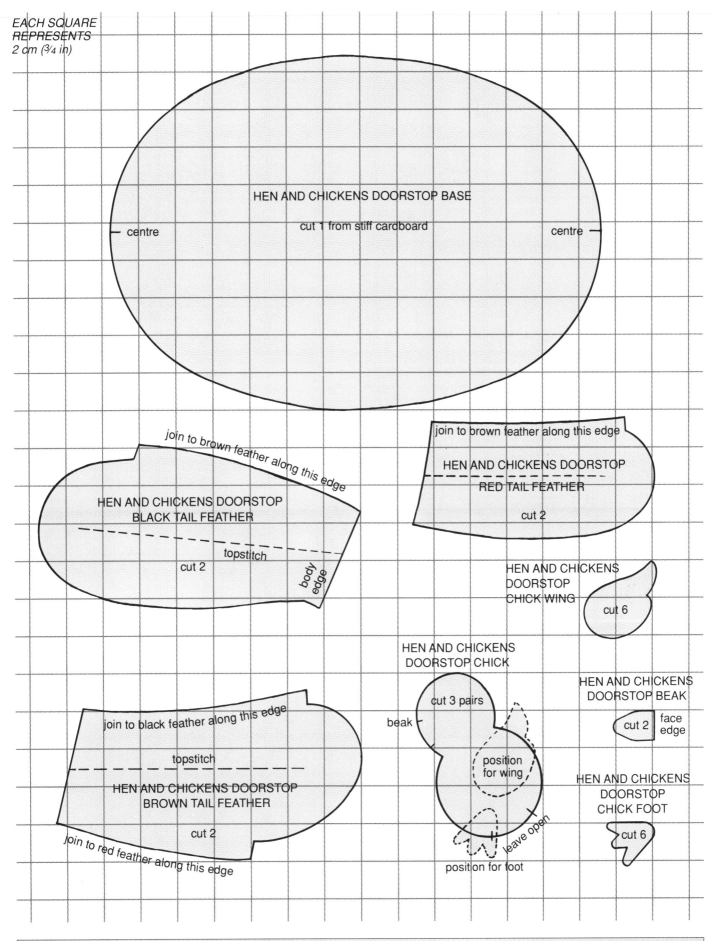

EACH SQUARE
REPRESENTS
2 cm (¾ in)

HEN AND CHICKENS DOORSTOP BASE

centre
cut 1 from stiff cardboard
centre

join to brown feather along this edge

HEN AND CHICKENS DOORSTOP
BLACK TAIL FEATHER

topstitch
cut 2

body edge

join to brown feather along this edge

HEN AND CHICKENS DOORSTOP
RED TAIL FEATHER

cut 2

HEN AND CHICKENS
DOORSTOP
CHICK WING

cut 6

HEN AND CHICKENS
DOORSTOP CHICK

cut 3 pairs

beak

position
for wing

leave open

position for foot

HEN AND CHICKENS
DOORSTOP BEAK

cut 2   face edge

HEN AND CHICKENS
DOORSTOP
CHICK FOOT

cut 6

join to black feather along this edge

topstitch

HEN AND CHICKENS DOORSTOP
BROWN TAIL FEATHER

cut 2

join to red feather along this edge

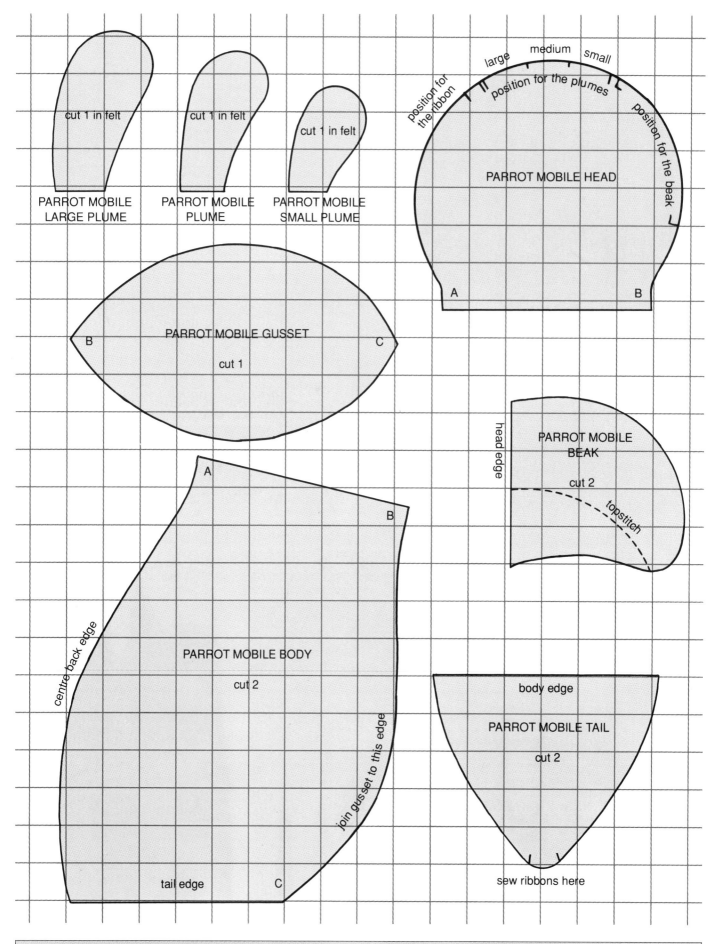

cut 1 in felt

PARROT MOBILE
LARGE PLUME

cut 1 in felt

PARROT MOBILE
PLUME

cut 1 in felt

PARROT MOBILE
SMALL PLUME

position for
the ribbon

large   medium   small

position for the plumes

position for the beak

PARROT MOBILE HEAD

A   B

B   PARROT MOBILE GUSSET   C

cut 1

head edge

PARROT MOBILE
BEAK

cut 2

topstitch

A

B

centre back edge

PARROT MOBILE BODY

cut 2

join gusset to this edge

body edge

PARROT MOBILE TAIL

cut 2

tail edge   C

sew ribbons here

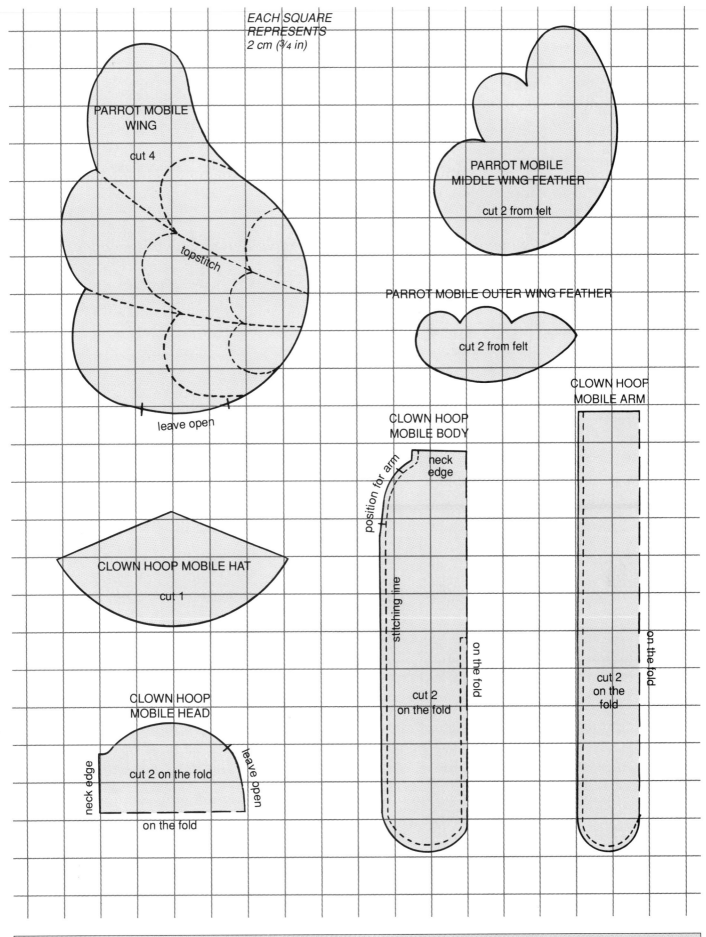

EACH SQUARE
REPRESENTS
2 cm (¾ in)

PARROT MOBILE
WING

cut 4

topstitch

leave open

PARROT MOBILE
MIDDLE WING FEATHER

cut 2 from felt

PARROT MOBILE OUTER WING FEATHER

cut 2 from felt

CLOWN HOOP
MOBILE ARM

CLOWN HOOP
MOBILE BODY

position for arm

neck
edge

stitching line

on the fold

cut 2
on the fold

on the fold

cut 2
on the
fold

CLOWN HOOP MOBILE HAT

cut 1

CLOWN HOOP
MOBILE HEAD

neck edge

cut 2 on the fold

leave open

on the fold

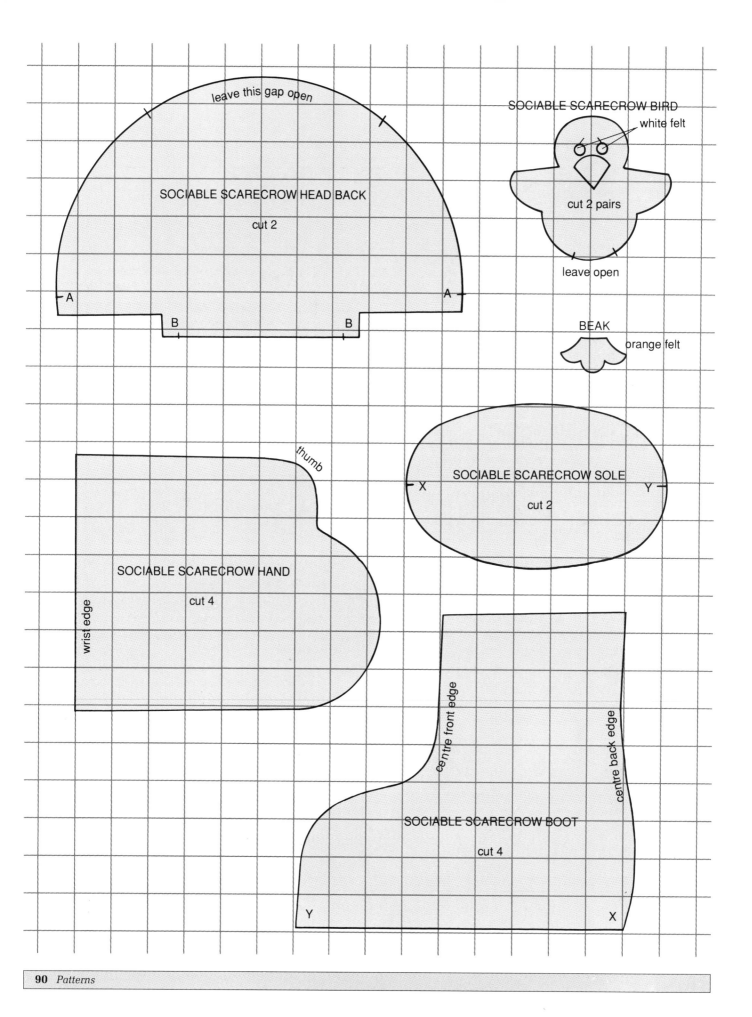

leave this gap open

SOCIABLE SCARECROW HEAD BACK

cut 2

A

B

B

A

SOCIABLE SCARECROW BIRD

white felt

cut 2 pairs

leave open

BEAK

orange felt

thumb

SOCIABLE SCARECROW SOLE

X

Y

cut 2

SOCIABLE SCARECROW HAND

cut 4

wrist edge

centre front edge

centre back edge

SOCIABLE SCARECROW BOOT

cut 4

Y

X

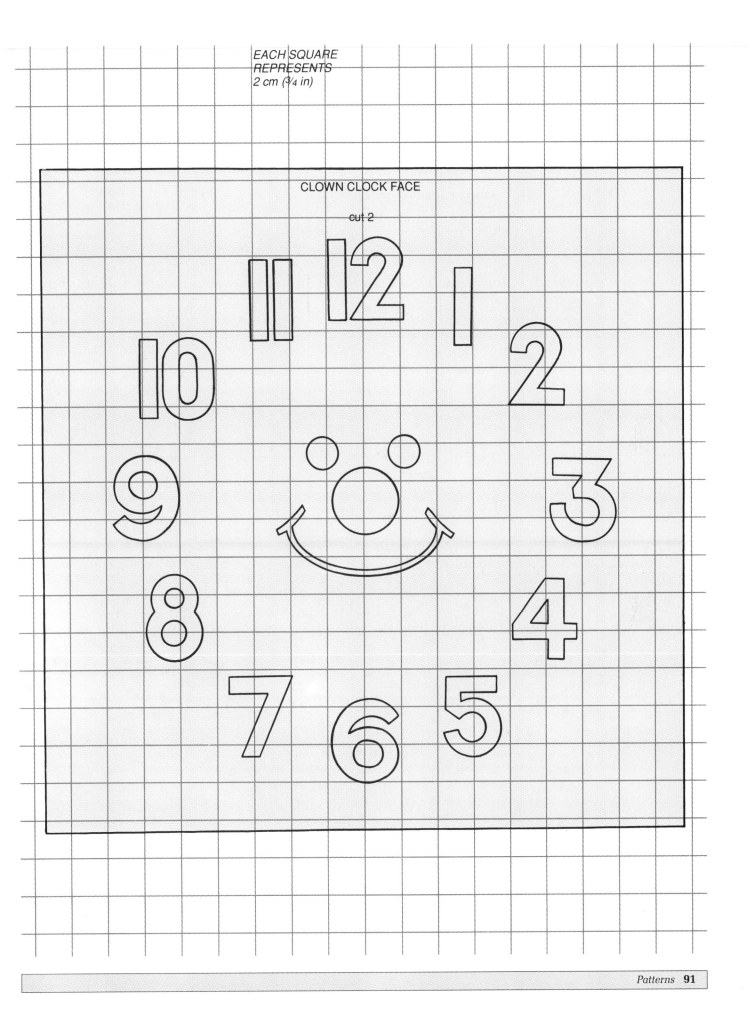

EACH SQUARE
REPRESENTS
2 cm (¾ in)

CLOWN CLOCK FACE

cut 2

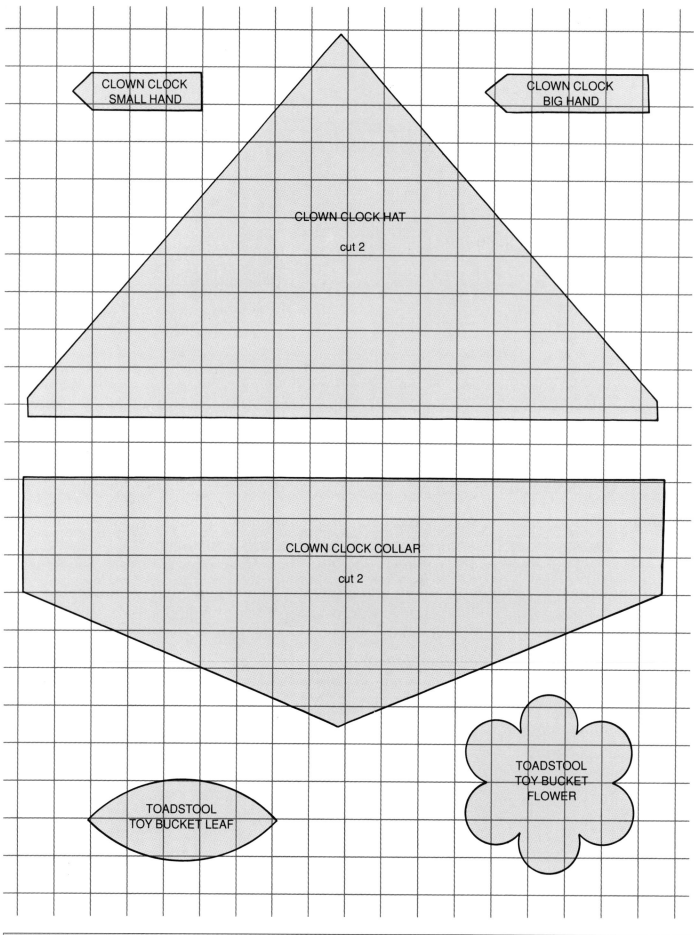

CLOWN CLOCK
SMALL HAND

CLOWN CLOCK
BIG HAND

CLOWN CLOCK HAT

cut 2

CLOWN CLOCK COLLAR

cut 2

TOADSTOOL
TOY BUCKET
FLOWER

TOADSTOOL
TOY BUCKET LEAF

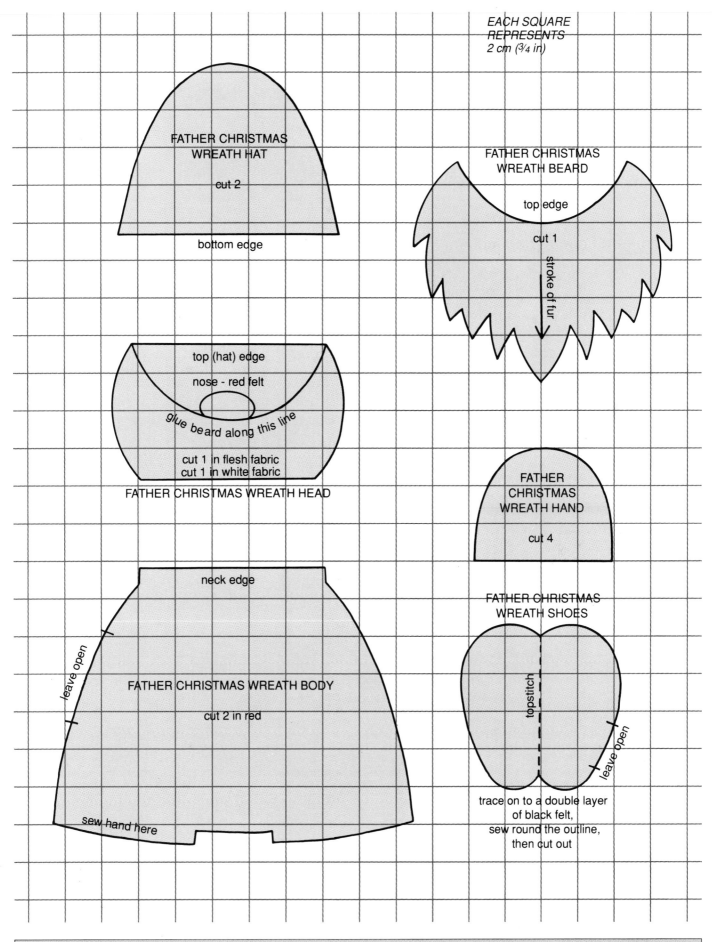

EACH SQUARE
REPRESENTS
2 cm (¾ in)

FATHER CHRISTMAS
WREATH HAT

cut 2

bottom edge

FATHER CHRISTMAS
WREATH BEARD

top edge

cut 1

stroke of fur

top (hat) edge

nose - red felt

glue beard along this line

cut 1 in flesh fabric
cut 1 in white fabric

FATHER CHRISTMAS WREATH HEAD

FATHER
CHRISTMAS
WREATH HAND

cut 4

FATHER CHRISTMAS
WREATH SHOES

neck edge

leave open

FATHER CHRISTMAS WREATH BODY

cut 2 in red

sew hand here

topstitch

leave open

trace on to a double layer
of black felt,
sew round the outline,
then cut out

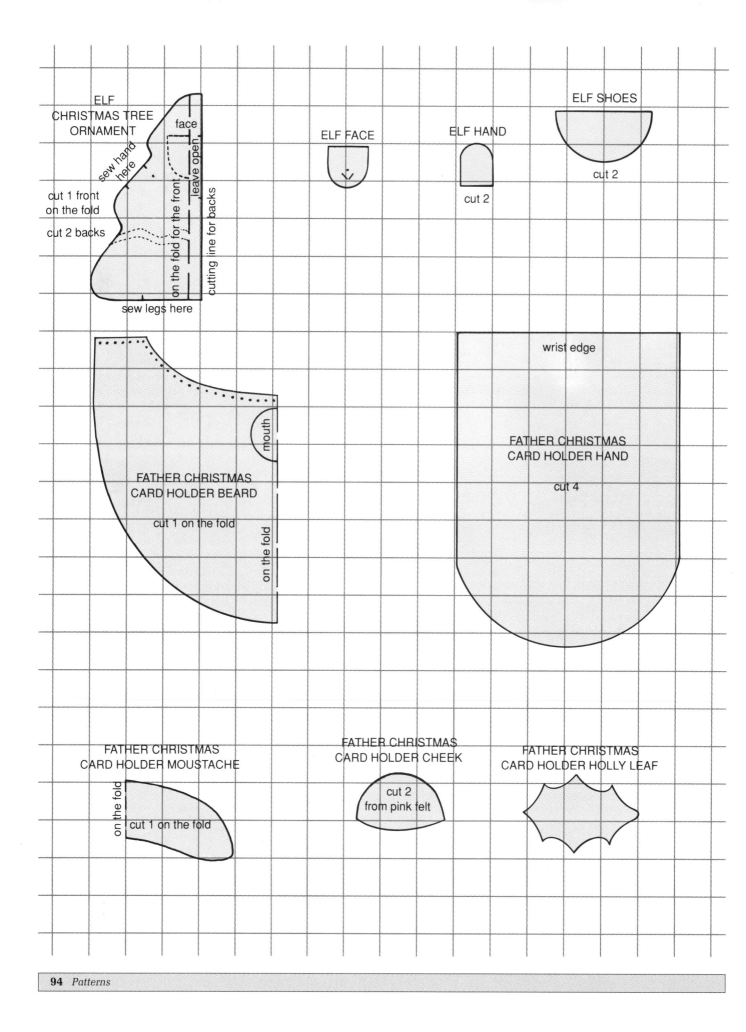

ELF
CHRISTMAS TREE
ORNAMENT

face

sew hand
here

leave open

cut 1 front
on the fold

cut 2 backs

on the fold for the front

cutting line for backs

sew legs here

ELF FACE

ELF HAND

cut 2

ELF SHOES

cut 2

mouth

FATHER CHRISTMAS
CARD HOLDER BEARD

cut 1 on the fold

on the fold

wrist edge

FATHER CHRISTMAS
CARD HOLDER HAND

cut 4

FATHER CHRISTMAS
CARD HOLDER MOUSTACHE

on the fold

cut 1 on the fold

FATHER CHRISTMAS
CARD HOLDER CHEEK

cut 2
from pink felt

FATHER CHRISTMAS
CARD HOLDER HOLLY LEAF

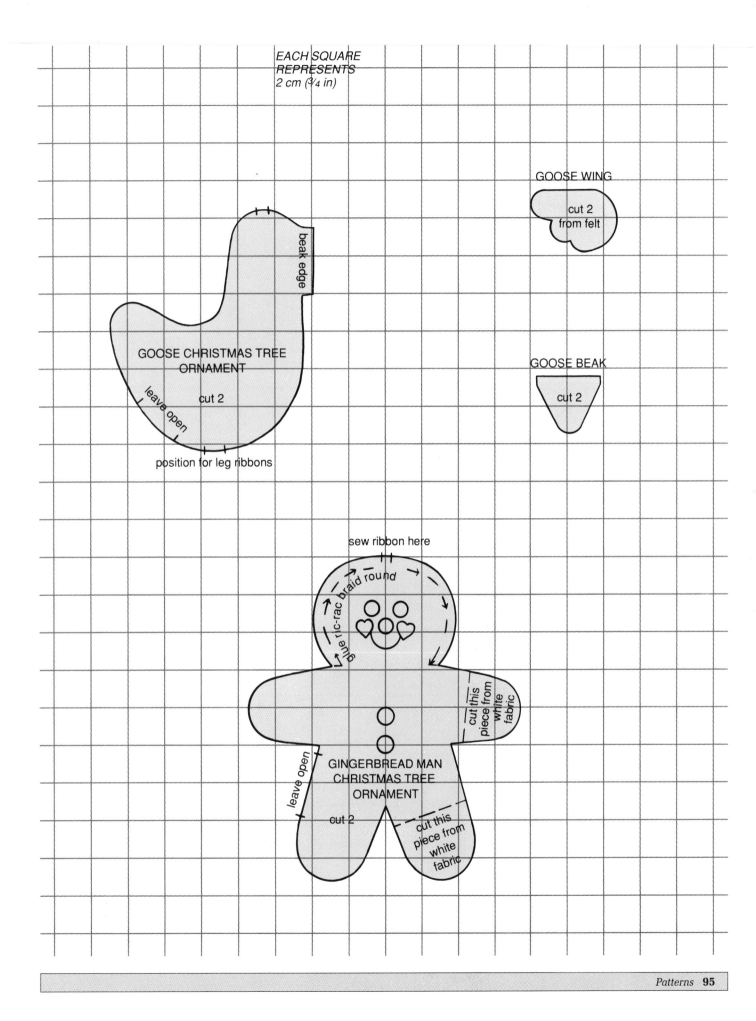

EACH SQUARE
REPRESENTS
2 cm (¾ in)

GOOSE WING

cut 2
from felt

beak edge

GOOSE CHRISTMAS TREE
ORNAMENT

cut 2

leave open

GOOSE BEAK

cut 2

position for leg ribbons

sew ribbon here

glue ric-rac braid round

cut this piece from white fabric

leave open

GINGERBREAD MAN
CHRISTMAS TREE
ORNAMENT

cut 2

cut this piece from white fabric